Understanding
Montessori

A Guide for Parents

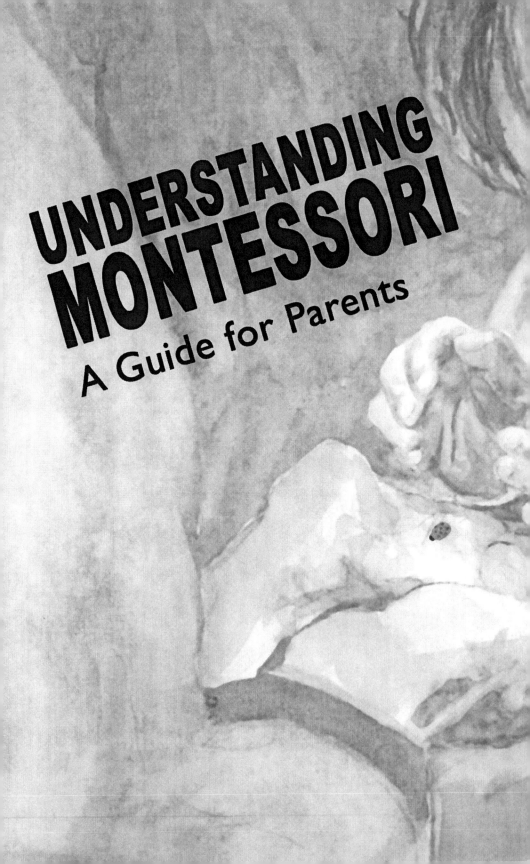

UNDERSTANDING MONTESSORI

MONTESSORI

A Guide for Parents

Maren Schmidt M. Ed.
with Dana Schmidt
illustrations by Syd Kruse

Excerpts from *The Secret of Childhood* by Maria Montessori are reprinted by permission of Random House, Inc.

Visit www.MarenSchmidt.com and www.KidsTalkNews.com

ISBN: 978-159858-974-0

This book is printed on acid-free paper.

Printed in the United States of America

Dedicated to
Pearl and Will Vanderwall
for their work as
humble servants to the child.

CONTENTS

Introduction

This book incubated in my nightstand drawer. My habit for many years has been to write goals and objectives and place them into my nightstand. As I transferred the accumulation of stuff from my old nightstand to a new one a few years ago, I discovered a goal written in 1996:

Help make Montessori education available to as many children as possible.

When I wrote this sentence in 1996, I was concerned about keeping tuition affordable at my school as we grew from twenty-eight students to almost a hundred students over the next twelve months. Reading this old goal in a different context made me think I had made no progress at all, as today "as many as possible" looks like millions.

Montessori education, more than anything, is about understanding and aiding the natural process of child growth and learning. The principles, methods, and materials used in Montessori education are scientifically supported, researched, and time-tested.

This goal took life again as I began to write a weekly newspaper column about child development, "Kids Talk," seeking to communicate to adults the child's point of view.

What my studies in brain and human development over the past five years illuminate, in conjunction with my twenty-five years of working with children, is this:

Authentic Montessori education is the most powerful way for children to learn in the world today.

Montessori education encompasses a culture that is innovative, respectful of the child, peaceful, joyful, collaborative, child-centered, community-minded, developmentally exacting, and supported by research. Montessori classrooms include the outdoors and aid children in valuing and caring for the wonders of our Earth.

Unfortunately, less than five percent of the children in the United States have an opportunity for a Montessori learning experience. I believe if parents understood the mightiness of Montessori education for their children and their families, they would find ways to create authentic Montessori education for their children, be it private, public, parochial, or home schools.

My daughter, Dana, and I conceived this book in February 2006, and together wrote eight chapters. We didn't find a method to have both of our voices in the book without creating a disjointed style. Dana's influence is here in her research with young parents, visiting classrooms, and helping me understand the needs of this new generation of parents. My voice and experience certainly dominate this book, but you should hear Dana's voice in the background asserting, "Mom, be sure to make this point."

This book is for parents. It's not meant to be a comprehensive study of Montessori education geared for teachers and administrators or a scholarly footnoted work, although I hope teachers and administrators will find the book helpful. This book expresses my understanding and experience of using Montessori principles for over twenty-five years. Others may have different experiences and perceptions. I share what worked for me.

My goal for this book is to help parents have a clear and concise resource for understanding Montessori educational principles and for finding a school situation, Montessori or not, that meets their family's needs. I want to explain Montessori education to parents against a backdrop of current research so parents can understand how and why Montessori education can benefit the lives of their children and families.

Parents are on the front lines of life, rearing children to become adults, taking care of their own parents, building careers, contributing to society through their work, and much more. The information in this book is my way of helping parents make informed decisions when time is in short supply.

Too many grandparents have commented to me, "I wish I had

known about Montessori education when my children were little." This book, I hope, will help parents understand the choices they have for educating their children.

As a guide for the future Dr. Maria Montessori, the Italian physician who developed Montessori education through her philosophy, methods and materials, asked us not to look to her, but to look at the child. Observing our children and helping our children meet their needs is the crux of Montessori education. Seeking and seeing the true nature of the child may be our most powerful help to all life on our planet.

By assisting a child we help parents and support families. As families are strengthened, our communities, our countries and our world become healthier places to live.

Look at the child. It is where everything begins.

Maren Schmidt
January 2009

Note to readers:

In common use, the term "Montessori" can be used as either a noun or an adjective depending on the context. At times this can be confusing.

In this book, when referring to Dr. Maria Montessori I will use the phrases Maria Montessori or Dr. Montessori. But "Montessori" can also be used alone, as a noun referring to the underlying philosophy of Dr. Montessori's work. An example would be the title of this book: "Understanding Montessori" or in the sentence: "Montessori uses multi-age classrooms."

As an adjective "Montessori" can describe classrooms, schools, methods, principles, techniques and more. In this book, when using "Montessori" as an adjective, I will follow it with the noun it modifies. For example: "Montessori schools are found all over the world."

When referring to Montessori teachers I use the pronoun "she" for simplicity's sake. There are many male Montessori teachers.

In *Chapter 10, Montessori Vocabulary Made Clear*, I define many Montessori specific terms. When these terms initially appear in this book, I italicize them.

When referring to specific Montessori materials, I capitalize the name, for example, the Red Rods or the Pink Tower.

The quotes from Dr. Montessori come from the book editions listed in the bibliography.

Chapter 1

So You Keep Hearing About Montessori

Fact or Fiction?

If you're like most people, odds are you've heard a lot of conflicting information about parenting. Friends, neighbors, family, and coworkers love to offer opinions about diapers, baby food, toilet training, television viewing, childcare, and preschools. You may have listened to glowing reports from others about how happy they are with their child's Montessori school, and a Montessori program sounds like something you should seriously consider. It's not unusual for children's preschools and elementary schools to be chosen based on the recommendations of others.

"Three of my friends have recommended your school to me," is a common first sentence in telephone calls from prospective parents at Montessori schools.

Then something happens to create doubt.

- You meet a "problem" child who goes to a Montessori school.
- A grandfather in the coffee shop says to you, "Montessori? Isn't that where the children run around and just do what they want?"
- A friend says that Montessori schools ask parents to donate thousands of dollars a year on top of tuition.

- Another says, "Montessori kids are horrible spellers."
- Someone tells you that Montessori schools create work-obsessed little soldiers.
- Another mentions that Montessori education is too laid-back and makes kids lazy.
- You notice a headline in *USA Today* about preschoolers being expelled from Montessori schools because of behavior issues. Are Montessori schools too strict?

We designed this book to help you sort fiction from fact so that you can make informed decisions about your children's education. If your child is currently enrolled in a Montessori program, we also hope this book will help further your understanding.

In this chapter we'll give an overview of two issues: what Montessori education is and is not.

There are many who hold, as I do, that the most important period of life is not the age of university studies, but the first one, the period from birth to the age of six. For that is the time when man's intelligence itself, his greatest implement, is being formed.

Maria Montessori

The Absorbent Mind, page 21

What Montessori Is

In its simplest form, Montessori refers to the philosophy of child and human development as presented by Dr. Maria Montessori, an Italian physician who lived from 1870 to 1952.

In the early 1900s, Dr. Montessori built her work with mentally challenged children on the research and studies of Jean Itard and Edward Seguin. Itard is known for his work with Victor, the "Wild Boy of Aveyron," an eleven-year-old found in the woods of France in 1799. Victor lacked spoken language skills and is presumed to have survived without human interaction. Itard's work established the idea that language can only be learned early in life. Itard also designed hands-on language materials for teaching Victor, materials that Dr. Montessori further developed.

Seguin expanded Itard's work with deaf children and designed hands-on materials for understanding basic mathematics. In 1907, at the behest of the Roman Association for Good Buildings, Dr. Montessori began using her teaching materials, based on Itard's and Seguin's designs, with normal children in a Rome tenement. Working with those children Dr. Montessori discovered what she called the "Secret of Childhood."

What is the secret? Children love to be involved in self-directed, purposeful activities. When given a *prepared environment* of meaningful hands-on projects, along with the time to do those projects at his or her own pace, a child will choose to engage in activities that will create learning in personal and powerful ways.

> **The Secret of Childhood? Children thrive on self-directed, purposeful activity.**

A Montessori prepared environment includes the outdoors as well as the indoors and is filled with time-tested, hands-on materials that meet specific learning needs and encourage positive brain development. Above all, Montessori prepared environments are attractive to children and peaceful, giving children a place to learn and grow in grace and dignity. The prepared environment is a key Montessori concept that we will discuss in further detail in *Chapter 4, How Does A Montessori Environment Work?*

Over the past hundred years Montessori classrooms all over the world have proven that, when correctly implemented, Dr. Montessori's philosophy, methods and materials work for children of all socioeconomic circumstances and all levels of ability. In a properly prepared Montessori classroom, research shows that children learn faster and more easily than in traditional classrooms.

However, the implementation of Montessori philosophy is a school's largest challenge. There are many factors to consider when putting Montessori theory into practice, for example: the children in the classroom; their ages and emotional well-being; parent support and understanding of Montessori philosophy; and, most important, the training and experience of teachers, assistants, and administrators.

Because of these factors, Montessori classrooms come in all shapes and sizes, from the small, in-home class for a few children to schools with hundreds of students with infants to, in some instances, high school.

While schools vary in size and scope, successful Montessori classrooms and schools will have three key components that create an *authentic Montessori* educational experience:

1. Adults professionally trained in Montessori philosophy, methods and materials for the group they are teaching
2. Prepared environments based on three-year age groups
3. Children's *free choice* of activity within a three-hour work cycle.

Chapter 2, Why Does the Montessori Method Work? examines the underlying philosophy of Montessori education. *Chapter 4, How Does a Montessori Environment Work?* focuses on methods and materials, as well as describes the children's activities in Montessori prepared learning environments. These two chapters, along with *Chapter 3, Montessori Principles, More than Teaching,* should present a clear picture of what Montessori education is.

Based on my personal experiences, I think it's valuable to know what Montessori is not. Before we go any further, I'd like to take some time to debunk some of the misconceptions that can prevent an accurate understanding of Montessori education.

What Montessori Is Not: Busting Montessori Myths

In my twenty-five years in Montessori education—as a parent, school employee, volunteer, trainee, teacher, school founder, and school director—I've come to new and deeper understandings of Dr. Montessori's insights into children and the process of human development and education.

My first encounter with Montessori schooling was less than positive. As a college student, I frequently visited my family after my four younger siblings' school day. Our family tradition was to have a snack together after school, and friends and neighbors were always welcomed.

The neighbor girls, ages four, five, and six, frequently joined the group. They would barge into my parents' house and head straight for the refrigerator—no knock on the door, no hello. They inhaled huge amounts of food with neither manners nor thanks. Their lack of decorum appalled me.

The girls' grandmother enjoyed telling us how wonderful the girls' Montessori school was and how much they learned there. I attributed the girls' ill-mannered conduct to their Montessori school. If a school would put up with that kind of behavior, I figured it couldn't be any good.

A few years passed, and I had children of my own. Our friends and coworkers recommended the local Montessori school to my husband and me. Because of my experiences with the neighbor children, I responded negatively to my friends' suggestions—very negatively.

I began to notice, though, that our friends' children were well mannered, articulate, and a joy to be around. Hum? So what was up with Montessori?

My mother helped clear up my misperceptions. The neighbor girls were suffering the effects of a newly divorced and stressed mother attending law school. The girls were starved for food, attention, and adult guidance. Their behavior was a reflection not of their Montessori school but of the turmoil in their home.

This showed me that what we may think are the effects, negative or positive, of a Montessori school may be something quite different.

Let me use my twenty-five years of Montessori experience to help dispel a few misconceptions about Montessori schools, some of which I've held myself.

Myth 1. Montessori schools are only for rich kids.

Many Montessori schools in the United States are private schools begun in the early to mid-1960s, a time when most public education didn't offer kindergarten, and only 5 percent of children went to preschool compared with the 67 percent reported in the 2000 census. When many Montessori schools were established, private preschools might have been options only for those in urban well-to-do areas. This exclusive availability may have given the impression that only wealthy families can afford Montessori school. The first schools that Dr. Montessori established were in the slums of Rome for children left alone at home while parents were out working and certainly not for rich kids.

In December 2008 in the United States there are 275 public Montessori schools and 120 charter Montessori schools that offer taxpayer-financed schooling. There are thousands of private not-for-profit Montessori schools that use charitable donations to offer affordable tuition. Homeschooling the Montessori way is an affordable alternative for some families.

Montessori education, through these low-cost options, is available to families interested in quality education. Many private Montessori schools offer scholarships, and some states offer childcare credits and assistance to low-income families. I've known more than one teenaged single mother who used government assistance to help pay for Montessori preschool while she went to college. Also, some Head Start programs have Montessori classrooms.

Montessori education can be affordable for families at most income levels.

Myth 2. Montessori schools are for smart kids.

Montessori education is for all children.

To the casual observer, Montessori students may appear advanced for their age, leading to the assumption that the schools cater to smart children. When three-year-olds begin working in a Montessori prepared learning environment, these children learn to read, write, and understand the world around them in ways that they can easily express to adults. When a child tells you that the corolla of a flower is purple, you might think she is much older than three or four. Learning the parts of the flowers comes naturally with the hands-on materials in the classroom and

Montessori teachers' language presentations.

Montessori schools offer children of differing abilities ways to express their unique personalities through activities using hands-on materials, language, numbers, art, music, movement, and more. Montessori schooling helps each child develop individuality in a way that accentuates his or her innate intelligence. Montessori schools can help make all kids smart kids.

Myth 3. Montessori schools are for the learning disabled.

It is true that Dr. Montessori began her work with children who were institutionalized due to physical or mental impairments. However, when using her methods and materials with normal children, Dr. Montessori discovered that children learned more quickly using her teaching methods.

This discovery is supported by recent research. For example, Dr. Angeline Lillard's research at Craig Montessori in Milwaukee showed that by the end of kindergarten Montessori students performed better than their peers at executive control, decoding language and early math, social awareness, and appeals to social justice. By sixth grade Montessori students outperformed their peers in social skills, exhibiting a sense of community, creativity in story writing, and complexity of sentence formulation.

There are some Montessori schools or classrooms that cater specifically to children who have learning challenges. In many Montessori schools, however, children with special needs are included in regular classrooms when those requirements can be met with existing school resources.

> *Maria Montessori discovered children learned more quickly using her methods.*

Myth 4. Isn't Montessori part of the Catholic Church?

Like many preschools, some Montessori schools may have church ties, but most Montessori schools are established as independent entities. Conversely, a school might be housed in a church building and not have any religious affiliation. Since Montessori refers to a philosophy and not an organization, schools are free to have relationships with other organizations, including churches.

Catholic or other religious organizations did establish some of the first Montessori programs. Dr. Montessori was Catholic and worked on developing "The Catechesis of the Good Shepherd," a hands-on church learning experience for young children. Dr. Montessori also used many biblical and religious references in her books, reflecting her classical education and the mores of that time. The Montessori movement, however, has no religious affiliations.

Montessori schools around the world reflect the specific values and beliefs of the staff members and families that form each school community. Around the world there are Montessori schools that are part of Catholic, Muslim, Jewish, and other religious communities.

Myth 5. Don't Montessori kids run around and do whatever they want?

When looking at a Montessori classroom, you will see twenty-five to thirty children involved in individual or small group activities. It is possible that you may see twenty-five children moving about the classroom involved in twenty-five different activities. At first glance, a classroom may look like a hive of bumblebees.

If you take the time to follow the activities of two children over the course of a three-hour work period, you will see a series of self-directed activities referred to as a *work cycle*. The children aren't running wild in the classroom. They are each involved in self-selected activities, which Montessorians refer to as *work*, designed to build concentration and support independent learning.

Choosing what you do is not the same as doing whatever you want. A well-known anecdote about Montessori students doing what they like comes from E. M. Standing's book, *Maria Montessori: Her Life and Work*.

A rather captious and skeptical visitor to a Montessori class once buttonholed one of the children—a little girl of seven—and said: "Is it true that in this school you are allowed to do anything you like?" "I don't know about that," replied the little maiden cautiously, "but I do know that we like what we do!"

The feelings that working in a Montessori classroom inspires might be reflected in the words of playwright and composer Noel Coward, "Work is much more fun than fun."

Myth 6. Montessorians seem like a selective sorority or clique.

One definition of clique is "an exclusive circle of people with a common purpose." Many *Montessori teachers* could be accused of this because of their intense desire to be of service in the life of a child coupled with the teacher's knowledge of child development. And while many school communities are close, they are not necessarily exclusive. You should look for a school where you and your family feel welcomed.

For many years *Montessori teacher training* was available only in a few larger cities, and becoming certified required prospective teachers to be determined and dedicated as relocating was often required. Now Montessori teacher's training is more accessible. Dozens of colleges and universities now offer undergraduate or graduate programs in Montessori education in conjunction with Montessori training centers. Loyola College in Maryland, New York University, Xavier University, and College of St. Catherine are only a few of the many institutions of higher learning that include Montessori teacher's training.

Dr. Montessori's books, full of Italian scientific and psychological terminology translated into the British English of the early 1900s, can be difficult for the modern reader to follow. To parents, the use of Montessori-specific terms and quotes may at times take on esoteric tones of an exclusive inner circle. The enthusiasm and dedication evident in the work of many *Montessorians* might be misinterpreted as excluding to uninitiated newcomers.

Understanding Montessori strives to demystify Montessori ideas and communicate the common sense and true inclusiveness of

Montessori philosophy and practice. In *Chapter 10, Montessori Vocabulary Made Clear*, we list and define specific terms to help you become familiar with key words before you visit your first school or pick up a volume of Dr. Montessori's essays.

Myth 7. Montessori classrooms are too structured.

Parents sometimes see the Montessori concept of "work as play" as too serious for preschoolers. The activities in the classroom are referred to as "work", and the children are directed to choose their work. However, the children's work is satisfying to them, and they make no distinction between work and play. Montessori activities are both interesting and fun to the child.

Each Montessori classroom is lined with low shelves filled with precise hands-on learning materials. The teacher, or *guide*, shows the children how to use the materials by giving individual lessons. The child is shown a specific way to use the materials but is allowed to explore the materials by using them in a variety of ways with a limitation being that the materials not be abused or used to harm others.

For example, the Red Rods, which are a set of ten painted wooden rods up to a meter long and about an inch thick, may not be used as Jedi light sabers. Obviously, sword fights with the Red Rods are a danger to other children as well as abusive to the rods, which cost about two hundred dollars a set.

In cases where materials are being damaged or used in a way that may hurt others, the child should be gently and kindly redirected to other work.

Unfortunately, some parents see this limitation on the use of the material as "too structured" since it may not allow for fantasy play. Choice in the Montessori classroom makes work into play.

Perhaps Mark Twain understood this concept when he wrote, "Work consists of whatever a body is obliged to do. Play consists of whatever a body is not obliged to do."

Myth 8. A Montessori classroom isn't structured enough for my child.

The Montessori classroom is structured, but differently from a traditional preschool. Dr. Montessori observed the normal or natural tendency of children to use self-selected, purposeful activities to develop themselves. The Montessori classroom, with its prepared activities and trained adults, is structured to promote this natural process of human development, a process Montessorians call *normalization*.

Students new to the Montessori classroom, who may or may not have been in a traditionally structured school, learn in about six to eight weeks to create their own work or success cycle. Montessorians refer to a child who creates his or her own work cycle as normalized, or using the natural and normal tendencies of human development.

Many traditional preschools work on a schedule where the entire classroom is involved in an activity for fifteen minutes then moves on to the next activity. This *structure* is based on the belief that young children have a short attention span of less than twenty minutes per activity. A typical morning at a traditional preschool might look something like this:

Traditional Preschool Schedule	
8:30 to 8:45	Morning circle and singing
8:45 to 9:00	Work with salt dough
9:00 to 9:15	Letter of the day work
9:15 to 9:30	Crayon work
9:30 to 9:45	Snack
9:45 to 10:15	Outdoor time
10:15 to 10:30	Story time
10:30 to 10:45	Work with Puzzles
10:45 to 11:00	Practice counting to 20
11:00 to 11:15	Craft project: cut out a paper flower
11:15 to 11:30	Circle time to dismissal

The above schedule reflects structure created by and dependent upon the teacher.

In the Montessori classroom, each child creates his or her own cycle of work based on individual interests. This cycle of self-directed activity lengthens the child's attention span. The teacher, instead of directing twenty children in one activity, quietly moves from child to child giving individual lessons with materials. The teacher or assistant may lead a few small group activities such as reading out loud, cooking, or gardening with two to six children.

In a Montessori classroom, a three-year-old's morning might look like this:

Montessori Preschool Schedule	
8:30 to 8:35	Arrive, hang up coat, and greet teacher
8:35 to 9:00	Choose Puzzle Map, work three times
9:00 to 9:30	Return puzzle to shelf, choose Sandpaper Numbers. Trace Sandpaper Numbers.
9:30 to 10:00	Return numbers. Choose Pink Tower.
10:00 to 10:15	Return tower to shelf, prepare individual snack, and eat snack with friend
10:15 to 10:30	Choose and work with scissor-cutting lesson
10:30 to 11:15	Choose and work with Knobbed Cylinders
11:15 to 11:30	Clean up time and group time with singing

The Montessori classroom is a vibrant and dynamic learning environment where structure is created by each child selecting his or her activity, doing it, and returning the activity to the shelf. After successful completion of a task, there is a period of self-satisfaction and reflection, and then the child chooses the next activity.

Montessorians call this rhythm of activity a *work cycle*. Stephen Covey, in *The 7 Habits of Highly Effective People*, refers to the habit of a work cycle as creating an upward spiral of growth and change. Covey describes a spiraling process of "learn-commit-do" that empowers us to move toward continuous improvement, both as children and adults.

If we turn to the House of Children we observe something strange. Left to themselves the children work ceaselessly; they do not worry about the clock. Another strange thing is that after long and continuous activity the children's capacity for work does not appear to diminish but to improve.

Maria Montessori

What You Should Know About Your Child, page 92

Myth 9. Montessori schools don't allow for play.

Montessorians refer to the child's activities in the classroom as work. The children also refer to what they do in the classroom as "their work." When your three-year-old comes home from school talking about the work he did today, he can sound way too serious for a kid you just picked up at preschool.

What adults often forget is that children have a deep desire to contribute meaningfully, which we deny when we regard everything they do as "just" play. With our adult eyes, we can observe the child's "joyful work" and expressions of deep satisfaction as the child experiences "work as play."

Consider this. You start a new job. You arrive the first day full of enthusiasm and ready to contribute to the success of your work group as well as your personal success. You're met at the door by your new boss and told, "Go outside and play. We'll let you know when it's time for lunch and time to go home."

Ouch!

But that's exactly what we do to our children when we dismiss their desires to contribute to their own well-being and to the common good of home or school.

Montessori schools create environments where children enjoy working on activities in grace and dignity. Children who have worked in a Montessori classroom tell of feelings of satisfaction and exhilaration that we might have considered as only play.

It's as Mark Twain, who wrote of boyhood in *Tom Sawyer* and *Huckleberry Finn*, said, "Work and play are words used to describe the same thing under differing conditions."

Another important component of Montessori education is the emphasis on nature education with outside activities that range from learning to recognize the parts of plants, to gardening, to caring for the outdoors, to caring for plants and animals, and much more. Montessori education promotes active exploration and understanding of nature.

Myth 10. Montessori doesn't allow for creativity.

Creativity means "to bring something into existence." First we have an idea. Then we use our imaginations, thoughts, and skills to bring these ideas into being. The Montessori classroom nourishes the creative skills of writing, drawing, painting, using scissors, modeling clay, gluing, and so forth, to enable the child to express his or her thoughts and ideas in genuine and unique ways.

When I was in kindergarten, we were all given a coloring sheet of a caboose. I colored my caboose green. My teacher told me that cabooses were red. As I looked around, all the other children's cabooses were red. My classmates laughed at my green caboose. My face burned with humiliation, but I knew that there were green cabooses.

Twenty-four years later, I saw another green caboose. This one was attached to the end of a Burlington-Northern train. "Yes!" I wanted to shout back to my kindergarten class. "See, there are green cabooses."

What does a green caboose have to do with creativity?

In kindergarten, I wasn't trying to be creative with my green caboose. I was only trying to express myself because I had seen a green caboose.

Montessori classrooms allow for safe self-expression through art, music, movement, and manipulation of materials and can be one of the most creative and satisfying environments for a child to learn to experiment and express his or her inner self.

Noted architect Maya Lin, who won the contest to design the Vietnam Memorial as a senior at Yale, said, "Sometimes I think creativity is magic; it's not a matter of finding an idea but allowing the idea to find you."

In Montessori classrooms, children have time to allow ideas to find them and the time to express those ideas.

Myth 11. Kids can't be kids at Montessori.

Somehow, our expectations as parents and our experiences of seeing children in temper tantrums in restaurants and stores create a view of children as naturally loud, prone to violent behaviors, disrespectful of others, clumsy, and worse.

In a well-running Montessori classroom, though, one might be inclined to think that kids aren't being kids.

When you see twenty-five to thirty children acting purposefully, walking calmly, talking in low voices to each other, carrying glass objects, reading, and working with numbers in the thousands, you might think the only way this behavior could occur was by children being regimented into it. I observed my daughter, Dana, then fifteen months old, moving serenely around her infant classroom. She sure didn't act that way at home.

As I watched Dana's *infant-toddler* class in action, I saw the power of this child friendly environment. As the children moved from activity to activity, day by day their skills and confidence grew. Lessons in *grace and courtesy* helped the children with social skills. "Please," "thank you," and "would you please" became some of these toddlers' first words.

When Dana was three, one of her favorite school activities was the green bean cutting lesson, which she remembers fondly. After carefully washing her hands, she would take several green beans out of the refrigerator, wash them, cut them into bite-sized pieces with a small knife, and arrange them on a child-sized tray. She would carry the tray around the classroom asking her classmates, "Would you like a green bean?" As they looked up from their work, the other children would reply, "Yes, please," or "No, thank you."

"I remember being so happy doing that work," Dana told me.

When given a prepared environment, a knowledgeable adult, and a three-hour work cycle, children show us that the natural state of the child is to be a happy and considerate person. A kid is most like a kid when he or she is engaged in the work of a Montessori classroom.

> *A kid is most like a kid when working in a Montessori classroom.*

Myth #12. If Montessori is so great, why aren't former students better known?

Most of us associate our career success with our colleges. Not too many people come out and say, "When I was three years old, I went to Hometown Montessori School, and that made all the difference."

Here are a few well-known people who remember their Montessori school connections and consider their experiences vital.

- Julia Child, the cook and writer who taught Americans to love, prepare, and pronounce French dishes, attended Montessori school.
- Peter Drucker, the business guru who has been said to be one of the most important thinkers of the twentieth century, was a Montessori student.
- Alice Waters, the chef of Chez Panisse fame and creator of The Edible Schoolyard project, was a Montessori teacher.
- Anne Frank attended a Montessori school and her famous diary was a natural extension of Anne's Montessori elementary school days where keeping a diary was encouraged.
- Larry Page and Sergei Brin, founders of Google, Jeff Bezos, founder of Amazon.com, and Steve Case of America Online, all credit Montessori schooling to their creative success.
- Annie Sullivan, Helen Keller's teacher, corresponded with Maria Montessori about teaching methods.

Montessori schools are focused on helping children become self-directed individuals who can and do make a difference in their families, in their communities, and in their world—famous or not.

And that's not a myth.

CHAPTER SUMMARY

Early in the twentieth-century, Dr. Maria Montessori developed and applied a philosophy of human development to education. Today, that philosophy supports a vibrant learning culture in Montessori schools worldwide. Dr. Montessori's principles, methods and materials are time-tested and uniquely effective.

Dr. Montessori discovered that children love to be engaged in self-directed, purposeful activities and learn best when involved in their self-chosen pursuits.

Authentic Montessori classrooms and schools have three common qualities:

- Adults professionally trained in Montessori philosophy, methods and materials for the age levels they teach.
- Prepared environments for each three-year age group.
- Children's free choice of activity within a three-hour-work cycle.

Montessori education is:

- For all socioeconomic groups, not just the well-to-do
- For all kids with all their gifts and learning challenges
- Child-directed so that the child creates his or her own structure of activities
- Non-sectarian
- Open to all
- Developmentally matched for every child
- For encouraging creativity
- For developing concentration through work as play
- Where children can be kids
- Designed to help children become self-directed individuals who make a difference

Chapter 2

Why Does the Montessori Method Work?

Meeting Needs

The simple reason the Montessori method works is that it meets the developmental needs of children.

With a traditional educational curriculum, one size must fit all. Such a curriculum is based more on the needs of adults than the needs of children. With Montessori theory and practice, each child creates a custom course of study through self-selected activities, guided by a trained Montessori teacher in a carefully designed learning environment.

The method is based on observing the activities of each child within a well-defined prepared environment of hands-on materials. Within the Montessori environment, children engage in activities of their choice using these materials during a three-hour work cycle. A trained adult observes and assists as appropriate, but it is the child's self-directed and purposeful activity that leads to greater *independence and concentration* as well as more rapid personal growth.

Fundamental concepts

The hands-on materials in a Montessori classroom have been carefully constructed based on fundamental concepts. The

25

materials and lessons in a Montessori classroom have been child-tested with children around the world, from all socio-economic backgrounds. Each lesson is designed to engage children's intellect through use of the hands and the five senses. Each lesson is also based on a set of foundational principles of human development.

Let's examine some of the elements taken into consideration for the creation of the child's activities in the Montessori prepared environment of a school.

- Four Planes of Development
- Human Tendencies
- Pedagogical Principles
- Prepared Environment
- Three-Hour Work Cycle
- Three-Year Age Span
- Concentration and Independence
- Free Choice
- Freedom within Limits
- Understanding Imagination, Creativity, and Fantasy
- The Work of the Hand and the Mind

As a young parent, at times I was completely confused at how I should approach child-rearing. I'd read in one book to do one thing, and the next day I'd read advice to do the complete opposite. My mother told me one thing and a neighbor something else.

In search of truth, I questioned the adults around me about how they had successfully parented. Uncle Norm and Aunt Charlotte joked that before having children they had ten theories on child-rearing. "Now we have ten children and no theories."

Often as parents we can feel as if finding clear direction for parenting is a sink-or-swim situation with nobody around to throw us a life preserver.

For me, discovering Montessori principles, philosophy, and practice felt as if I'd been thrown a life vest, a lifeboat, and a year's supply of rations, along with a book called *How to Survive on a*

Deserted Island...With Children.

Dr. Montessori's principles provide an understanding of children from birth through *adolescence* using a consistent and practical commonsense approach. Understanding about the *four planes of development* is a big help.

Four Planes of Development: A Human Growth Continuum

Dr. Montessori first discussed the four planes of development at the Edinburgh lectures in 1938, over thirty years after beginning the first classroom in the Roman slums of San Lorenzo. Montessori said, "We have been guided by the manifestation of children at different stages of growth. Each may be considered a level or plane. On each different level of life, there are different needs and different manifestations."

Dr. Montessori saw that each stage or plane of development had unique characteristics and that each level prepared the child for the next period of development. Our children are on a *continuum of development.*

As parents and adults, we can observe our children engaged in their chosen activities and by using Montessori principles, can gain powerful insights into our children's personalities and developmental needs.

Just as a butterfly has unique needs during each stage of metamorphosis, from egg, larvae, chrysalis, and emerging adult, our children's requirements change over time.

At the end of each plane or stage, the child's psychological makeup changes along with physical characteristics. Dr. Montessori considered this a rebirth in the development of the child. In our diagram for the four planes of development the line drawn at the end of each plane signifies this major life change.

A plane consists of two sub-stages, each approximately three years in duration. In the first sub-stage of each plane, change is rapid. In the second sub-stage, growth is slower and more stable.

First plane of development

From birth through the sixth year, the child is sensitive to the acquisition of certain skills and knowledge, among these being language, movement, social relations, refinement of sensory perceptions, and an understanding of order. Dr. Montessori referred to these times for learning as *sensitive periods*. We'll talk more about sensitive periods in *Chapter 3, Montessori Principles: More Than Teaching* and in *Chapter 10, Montessori Vocabulary Made Clear.*

From birth to six years, the child is an unconscious learner. A perfect example of this is that under normal circumstances we don't have to teach a child how to walk or talk. The child is not aware of learning but appears drawn to activities that develop skills in talking, movement, interaction with people, tasting, smelling, hearing, seeing, touching, and creating order from all the information he or she is gathering. A child's choices for activities center on individual construction and personal mastery.

The theme of the first plane of development might be seen in our children's request to "let me do it myself" as they learn to feed themselves, use the toilet, blow their noses, and a thousand other skills.

Around the time the first baby tooth is lost and adult teeth emerge, the child's brain changes along with learning needs.

Second plane of development

For the child ages six to twelve years, we refer to the sensitive periods of development as *psychological characteristics*. The child's activities are now focused around:

- Getting out of the narrow circle of family and close friends
- Expanding intellectual horizons
- Building up of a sense of morality
- Using the imagination
- Working in a group instead of alone
- Developing a reasoning mind
- Becoming a conscious learner
- Experiencing an extremely healthy period of life

During this stage of development, we'll hear our children complain that certain activities are "boring." The knock-knock and

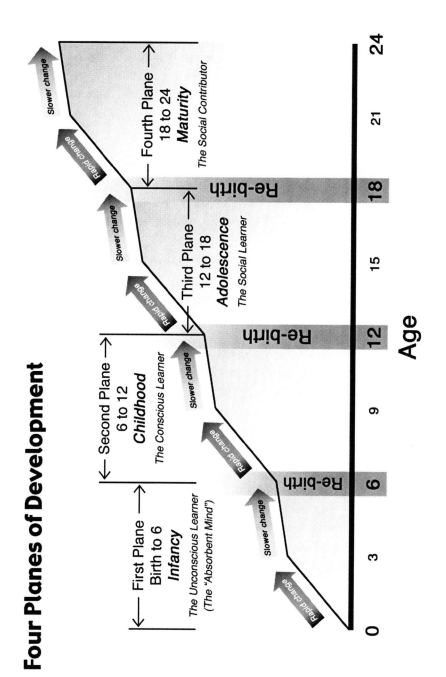

Four Planes of Development

First Plane → Birth to 6 *Infancy*
The Unconscious Learner
(The "Absorbent Mind")

← Second Plane 6 to 12 *Childhood*
The Conscious Learner

Third Plane 12 to 18 *Adolescence*
The Social Learner

Fourth Plane 18 to 24 *Maturity*
The Social Contributor

Re-birth

Rapid change

Slower change

Age

elephant jokes start, as do the requests to spend the night at friends' homes. At this age our children are also developing a moral sensibility, and the phrase "that's not fair" is frequently used. Also, children will ask to learn certain skills or study specific subjects, for example riding a bike or learning about Egyptian history.

As the child enters puberty, around age twelve, a new set of learning proclivities emerge.

Third plane of development

The needs and manifestations for the child from ages twelve to eighteen change. Some of these follow:

- Rapid physical growth, sexual maturation, boundless energy
- Newly developing intellectual capabilities: abilities to abstract, conjecture, predict, and create
- Need to be with peers, and to be accepted, as well as a need for mentor relationships with adults who are not their parents
- Need to form personal identity—the adolescent wants to know "What am I good at?" and "What am I good for?"
- Developing self-awareness, uncertainty, emotional unevenness—adolescence is a self-critical age
- Need for meaningful work that contributes to their communities
- Need to express their new interests, thoughts, and emotions, to acquire flexible and inquiring habits of the mind, to develop a personal vision

The young teenager begins to create his or her own "we generation." Young teens change rapidly to adapt to this need to belong to their time and place, thus becoming contemporaries. This is one reason we can look at old high school pictures and pinpoint the year based on the fashions at the time.

The young teen needs to argue, disagree, and oppose others, especially parents, teachers, and other authority figures. These teens push the envelope testing what is acceptable in our culture and what behavior or ideas are negotiable or flexible.

Poetry is a strong interest for a person this age. Often this is the only time in our lives that we read or write poetry. Finding powerful words for self-expression is important to the teen.

Self-expression is also seen in the teen's ongoing efforts to be in the leading edge of trends whether those trends be about hair color, fashion, computers or cell phones.

As parents of adult children will testify, this too shall pass, and a new set of learning needs emerge in the young adult.

Fourth plane of development

For ages eighteen to twenty-four years, Dr. Montessori saw this age person as being ready for a new period of self-construction by going out into world and creating his or her own experiences. At this time there are no Montessori environments that are specifically designed to meet the needs of this period. The young adult takes on the challenge of starting college, creating new life experiences through relationships and travel, and embarking on career and married life.

Another idea about the fourth plane is that we don't mature into adulthood until after the age of twenty-four. Recent research is corroborating this idea through changes in the brain seen in functional MRI scans. UCLA researchers, using MRI scans, compared the changes in the frontal lobes of teens and young adults. The researchers saw that the frontal lobes, which are involved in planning, impulse control and reasoning, were more mature in young adults than those in teens. This study suggests that the brain has not matured fully until the mid-twenties.

My vision of the future is no longer of people taking exams and proceeding on that certification from the secondary school to the university, but of individuals passing from one stage of independence to a higher, by means of their own activity, through their own effort of will, which constitutes the inner evolution of the individual.

Maria Montessori

From Childhood to Adolescence, Preface

Human Tendencies

The activities that have been developed in Montessori classrooms over the past hundred years are based on observable *human tendencies* toward certain behaviors. Humans have natural, observable patterns of behavior, or tendencies. Just as birds have a natural tendency to build nests and bees tend to build hives, humans, too, have tendencies.

These are the uniquely human characteristics that define us as being homo sapiens. A list of these tendencies follows:

Activity	Communication
Becoming	Imagination
Belonging	Exactness
Exploration	Repetition
Orientation	Perfection
Order	

This list may not include all tendencies but is meant to serve as a lens through which to view our children's motivations, needs, and behaviors.

The human tendency towards *activity* is easily seen through the wide variety of activities we each do each day and how difficult it is for most people to sit and do nothing. Our children are born to be active.

The tendency to *become* refers to the innate human tendency to learn and grow. Children naturally love to learn and feel like they are becoming bigger. How proud children are to hold up another finger on their birthdays.

The human tendency to *belong* is evident in our desire to belong to our families, our communities, and be part of the world in the time and place where we are born and live.

Humans are explorers. Our *explorations* help us understand the world. Children have to explore their immediate environment to learn. Common sense as well as current brain research tells us that engaged exploration using all our senses is critical to optimal learning.

> **Engaged exploration using all our senses is critical to optimal learning.**

As we explore, we have to *orient* ourselves to our surroundings. When things change, we immediately work to re-orient ourselves to the situation. It's a natural tendency.

Humans like to impose *order* on their surroundings. Children appreciate the inherent order of a Montessori classroom as the materials they work with can be consistently found in the exact same spot, day after day. Learning is enhanced by tapping into this natural desire for order.

We can't stop children from learning how to talk. *Communication* is thought by many linguists to be hard-wired into the brain. By our very natures, humans cannot *not* communicate. Even if we don't say a word, nonverbally we communicate through gestures, appearance, and situational context.

Imagination is the human ability to visualize what is not directly in front of us. We use our imaginations to create as well as fill in missing information. Our tendency towards imagination causes us to design millions of things from songs to buildings, as well as see monsters under our beds.

Humans tend towards *exactness*. We mimic the gestures, clothing styles, and verbal idiosyncrasies of our group in an unconscious manner. Look at family reunion pictures and notice what similar colors family members wear even though there were no requests for certain colors or styles.

Repetition is another human tendency, especially in the young child. The child loves to repeat the same activities and routine day after day, establishing an order and orientation for learning and growth. In the older child and adult, repetition needs variation. Younger children are happy to watch the same movie every day for a month, as well as sing the same songs. I thought our Smurfs songs tape would never wear out! Older children and adults would rebel at watching the same movie twice in a row but would be happy to watch a different movie every day.

The tendency towards *perfection* is very human. Aren't we always trying to build a better mousetrap? Our children work to perfect movement, speech, and other basic skills. It is part of their natural human drive.

The lessons given in the prepared environments of a Montessori school are designed based on these human tendencies along with the sensitive periods and psychological characteristics for that age person—pretty potent stuff. Children's brains love it as well as their bodies, hearts, and social beings.

This leads us to our next element of why a Montessori classroom works: *pedagogical principles.*

Pedagogical Principles

You've just got to love the phrase "pedagogical principles." I had never heard of the terms pedagogy or pedagogical until I started learning about Montessori principles. Now I appreciate the subtleties of the word. Pedagogy means teaching and a lot more. Pedagogy includes teaching and learning, which aren't the same things at all.

A few years ago I read about a community college that was undergoing a "paradigm shift." The article quoted the school's president: "We will become a learning institution instead of a teaching institution."

For a few minutes I puzzled over the difference between a learning institution and a teaching institution. Then I figured out what the school's president was trying to say. The college was changing its emphasis to students learning instead of teachers teaching. Apparently teachers weren't helping students to learn.

> **Pedagogy includes teaching and learning, which aren't the same things at all.**

Here is a fundamental Montessori difference: Montessori teachers focus on and direct student learning. This is in contrast with traditional teaching where the main emphasis is determining if a child passes or fails what has been taught. The Montessori teachers' credo is "to be a help to life." Making sure a child succeeds in learning is a huge help in life. Montessori teachers are dedicated to guiding human development to ensure learning.

Pedagogy means the activities of educating, or, in other words, teaching or instructing activities that impart knowledge or skill. Here are some of the Montessori pedagogical principles, or teaching fundamentals, that ensure learning:

- Knowledge of human tendencies
- Awareness of psychological characteristics and sensitive periods
- Special Montessori prepared environments
- Limitation of material
- Teacher as link between child and the environment
- Freedom of choice and development of responsibility
- Auto-education or self-construction
- Whole to the parts; concrete to abstract
- The working of the hand and the mind
- Isolation of difficulty
- Observation of the child at work
- Repetition through variety
- Indirect preparation
- Techniques that lead to mental and physical independence

We'll discuss these techniques in greater detail in *Chapter 3, Montessori Principles: More Than Teaching*. Let's look at another key reason of why Montessori education works, the prepared environment.

The Prepared Environment

I never teach my pupils; I only attempt to provide the conditions in which they can learn.
    Albert Einstein

With the knowledge of the four planes of development, sensitive periods, human tendencies, and pedagogical principles, we need to create an ideal environment to maximize children's learning experience. Just as restaurants create special surroundings for their customers' needs, Montessori schools create specific environments to serve the needs of the children. Each classroom environment contains the activities for a three-year period of development and should contain a full complement of Montessori materials.

I always delight when watching a three-year-old enter a Montessori classroom for the first time. The child, more often than not, lights up, takes a deep breath, and looks up eyes wide in gratitude to his or her parents and to the Montessori teacher. "This is all for me?" the child says, a phrase I've heard many times on that initial visit.

Children intuitively know that the Montessori environment is all for them. This understanding is aided by the transparent organization of a Montessori classroom.

An environment with transparent organization provides children with an essential element of protection, which means safety from physical or psychological injury. Children seem to sense this built-in protection immediately in the child-sized and child friendly design of a Montessori space.

Children, in my experience, seem to perceive that the design of the classroom, with its shelves full of enticing, hands-on materials, provides a framework of ongoing challenges for individual learning.

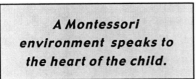

A Montessori environment speaks to the heart of the child.

The environment speaks to the heart of the child, non-verbally communicating that here is a place where a small being can work in peace and dignity, without fear of being hit or of being called names by the other children. The environment says to the child, "Here is a place where you will be understood and where you can grow and learn."

I've watched my former students at age twelve or older enter the classroom where they worked when they were three, four, and five years old. These tween-agers would be full of smiles and squeals of delight as they touched and worked with the familiar lessons and materials from their early childhood days. I'm confident that a Montessori environment continues to speak and support children's learning for many years after they have left.

The prepared environments in our Montessori schools involve

three basic elements: physical, order, and human. These basic elements provide both clear structure and expectations for the children, a structure that helps create a lifetime love of learning.

The physical element of a Montessori classroom

The physical space of the environment allows children to know that they have a place of their own to live and work. The physical elements communicate to the children that they belong. Child-sized tables, chairs, and activities allow children a certain dignity that increases with the growth of independence in the child.

Cleanliness, light, fresh air, and a comfortable temperature also communicate to the children an important sense of place. Crawl around on the floor in your home, and you might find that it's not as tidy as you thought and that the space in the "land down under the table" doesn't have the same light, air flow, or temperature of the space three feet above it. All aspects of Montessori classrooms are designed at child level.

Movement is allowed in a Montessori classroom, and the consequences of movement are permitted. If you bump a chair, it will make a noise against the floor. If you drop a glass flower vase, it may break. The consequences of movement help the child learn to make careful adjustments to his or her behavior without a teacher's intervention.

The limits to the child's space are well defined with areas for work with water, snack, art, large motor skills, and more. Access to the outdoors is available, and in many Montessori classrooms the line between indoors and outdoors is fluid with children going outside as they choose.

The importance of the physical aspect of a classroom is perhaps best seen in its absence. My college calculus class met in a temporary building that had seven-foot ceilings and the standard college student desks. Steve, a college friend who stood six feet eight, contorted himself into the desks and tried to avoid hitting his head on the door jambs and ceiling fans. My neck hurts just remembering this. To write on the chalkboard, Steve bent like a question mark. To pull off a sweater, Steve got on his knees so his arms wouldn't hit the ceiling. Just as Steve was oversized in a smaller world, our children deal with similar discomforts and indignities for many years in an oversized world.

A Montessori prepared environment fits the physical needs of children.

Order in the Montessori classroom

The idea of order might be summed up as "a place for everything and everything in its place." Order might seem obvious to organized people. Kitchen items in the kitchen. Car tools in the garage. Let's look at the different expressions of order in Montessori *primary classrooms,* designed for children three to six years old.

First, material is grouped by area and sequence, and areas are defined for different activities. There are five basic areas in a primary classroom: Practical Life, Sensorial, Mathematics, Language, and Cultural. As you look around the classroom, there will also be places for eating, for movement, for quiet reflection, and for art projects.

The *outdoor classroom,* depending on the school, will have tools and materials for gardening, sweeping, raking, composting, and other activities.

There is also order in each activity. As you look at each area, you will see that each activity is self-contained. For example, in the *practical life* area, all the items a child needs to polish shoes are on a tray, ready to be used. The teacher's presentation for shoe polishing gives the child a precise way to place the items outside of the tray, how to do the activity, and how to return it to order, leaving the activity ready for the next person.

Order is evident in that there is order in the sequence of activities. When you look at the area and shelf where the shoe polishing lesson is placed, to the left you will see a variety of activities that the child has done before coming to the work of shoe polishing.

Five-year-old Jane told me, "I need to do all the lessons on this shelf before I'll be ready to go to the elementary class." The children perceive the order and sequence in the classroom, either consciously like Jane or unconsciously as they ask for the next lesson on the shelf. In this sequencing of activities, children can visualize and thus realize their opportunities for personal growth.

> **Montessori classrooms create a sense in children of becoming more self-reliant.**

There is order in the life of the group. "I remember when I couldn't tie my shoes," five-year-old Ben told his three-year-old sister as he tied her shoes. "You'll learn how to tie shoes, too."

Montessori classrooms create a sense in children of becoming more self-reliant, day by day, year by year.

People in the Montessori classroom

A Montessori environment has a human dimension that includes adults and children. The adult's role in providing structure is to direct the child's activities and to prepare those activities. In these activities, the adult needs to *respect* the child as a fellow human being.

The adult observes the child's interaction with the world and looks for concentration and independence in the child. The adult's role in a Montessori classroom may seem simplistic: protect the few rules of basic order for the child and keep the environment clean and neat. The teacher makes sure that the activities for the child are easily accessible and are in good working order, that all parts are intact, and that the activities are attractively displayed. Sometimes the simple is the most difficult item to achieve.

The teacher is a role model. Adults, not only teachers, model to children what it means to be an adult. We need to be careful of our appearance, keeping healthy and rested, along with staying interesting to the child by pursuing personal

> **The adult is the most critical element of a child's environment.**

interests. If we neglect our own personal growth through various intellectual and physical activities, we neglect to model the vitality of being an adult to our children.

Remember the human tendencies toward exactness and

perfection? "Little pitchers have big ears," was a saying when I was growing up, and it's true today. Children hear and see more than we think they do. Children mimic our gestures, attitudes and words. Everything we do and say is extremely interesting to children. We need to remember that.

The work of the children in the classroom creates a vibrant and dynamic force that I call the popcorn effect. With enough children and an even age mix, the classroom becomes an interesting and engaging place for ideas, work, and positive social interchange. In my experience, I'd rather have too many children in a classroom than too few. With plenty of children, the energy in the classroom pops, and there seems to always be something interesting and fun to do. With too few children in a classroom, the learning dynamics change and may come to depend too heavily on adults.

The child's role in life is to self-construct an adult—an amazing feat. In our Montessori classrooms, we assist children by providing as unambiguous a system as possible so that the child is successful in becoming an adult with, in the words of Dr. Montessori, "an eye that sees, a soul that feels, and a hand that obeys."

Our leadership is at the core of true learning and self-discovery for our children. Our challenge as parents and teachers is to guide the whole person—the physical, the mental, the emotional, and the social being. Our challenge is that we must model the physical self-discipline, the vision that comes from mental exercise, the passion that speaks from the heart, and the conscience that reflects the spirit of our social being.

As we teach our children, we walk a path with them of trust, helping them to understand how to live their lives, how to develop their talents, how to share their love, and how to do what's right. This gift of a Montessori classroom—the freedom to choose activities that promote personal physical, mental, social, and moral growth—is a strength of the Montessori method.

Corrections strive to be of loving intention to serve the needs of the child. If a child is working a puzzle, Montessori teachers don't interrupt and say, "No, no, no. That piece goes there. Oh, is that too hard for you? Why don't you get something else to do?"

A Montessori teacher observes and assists, either through direct or indirect means, only when the child cannot do a task independently. Any unnecessary help is a hindrance to a child's personal development.

> *Any unnecessary help is a hindrance.*

In *Chapter 4, How Does A Montessori Environment Work?*, we'll further describe the prepared environments for the first three planes of development, or from birth to age eighteen.

Wouldn't it be lovely to have teenagers who see a problem, devise a solution, do it, and leave the situation better off than before? With no one asking? People report that's what they see with Montessori students.

The prepared environment of a Montessori classroom with its clear design of space, activities and people act as a true help to life, at all stages of development.

Three-Hour Work Cycle

The Montessori method works because the child is given the luxury of uninterrupted time. The child, engaged with free-choice activities during a *three-hour work cycle*, develops *independence and concentration* that aid in personal growth—mental, physical, emotional, and social—at all levels.

> *The gift of uninterrupted time is a strength of the Montessori program.*

In a Montessori classroom, we endeavor to give the child enough time and freedom to make his or her own choices for activities that hold personal meaning and significance. This freedom allows children to be children in powerful ways. These self-selected and self-directed activities help the child create a unique human being, a person of his or her own time and place.

We'll talk more about the three-hour work cycle in *Chapter 5, What? No Grades?* and explain in further detail how the three-hour work cycle contributes to personal growth at all levels.

Understanding the Three-Hour Work Cycle

Tired and agitated, Sara got ready for bed. What had happened to the day? She had woken up fresh that morning, ready to have a productive day.

During breakfast, Sara's assistant called to alert Sara that she wouldn't be in to copy the reports for the next day's meeting. When Sara went to make copies of her presentation, the toner cartridge was low, the paper jammed, and the machine ran out of staples.

When Sara reviewed the copies, page 17 had been skipped by the machine. Sara's lunch appointment cancelled while Sara was waiting in the restaurant. After lunch, she couldn't get online to do some research. Then Ron, a coworker, came in and complained about his weekend for half an hour.

What went wrong with Sara's day? Sara was unable to get a work cycle completed. A work cycle consists of selecting an activity, doing it, achieving some internal satisfaction for the work, then selecting the next task.

When we experience this cycle of "choose-do-return to order-satisfaction, then choose again," we create a powerful success cycle with feelings of accomplishment and contentment.

When we are having a productive work cycle, we'll say we are "on a roll." We go from task to task, choosing progressively harder tasks as time allows. On those high-achieving days, we feel unstoppable.

Then there are the days when we get off to fits and starts because we are interrupted, don't have enough time to complete a task before another commitment, or we lack the necessary supplies. How that trip to the hardware store can sabotage the best efforts for a productive workday.

Most of us, even small children, have a built-in, three-hour work cycle. We might contrast and compare it to our sleep cycle. When we know we have at least three hours of uninterrupted time, we will tackle a multitude of jobs and enjoy doing them.

If our time is interrupted, we may not even try to start anything. "It's not worth the effort," or "I don't feel like doing anything," we might say. Sound familiar?

When given a regular three-hour period, children (and adults) learn to tap into a success cycle. After accomplishing a series of short and familiar tasks in a ninety-minute time frame, a child will choose a task that is challenging and represents true learning. At this ninety-minute mark, there is a period of restlessness that lasts about ten minutes, until the choice for the challenging activity is made. The new activity may last for sixty to ninety minutes.

Here's an example of a recent Saturday morning three-hour work cycle for me—not very glamorous, but I was on a roll.

Clean kitchen, fifteen minutes. Start laundry, fifteen minutes. Make phone calls for appointments, twenty minutes. Vacuum, twenty minutes. Feeling of restlessness. What should I do next? Cup of coffee, ten minutes. Balance bank statements and pay bills, ninety minutes.

Here's an example of a four-and-a-half-year-old's work cycle that I recently observed. Work puzzle, ten minutes. Build with blocks, fifteen minutes. Water plants, twenty minutes. Sweep floor, ten minutes. Number counting cards, fifteen minutes. Walk up and down steps, five minutes. Talk with dad, ten minutes. Do a hundred-piece puzzle, forty-five minutes. Practice tying shoes, forty-five minutes.

When we have achieved a three-hour work cycle, normally we are eager to begin the next cycle. Productive adults have two to four work cycles a day. Children under the age of five usually have one work cycle a day. Around five, children will start a second work cycle if given the opportunity.

The gift of uninterrupted time gives us, children and adults, the opportunity to engage in our own powerful three-hour work cycles, creating personal success in learning, concentration, and independence.

Three-Year Age Span

In the primary classroom, the age span is normally referred to as "from three- to six-years old." But since each child develops on his or her own schedule, a primary classroom can have children as young as two-and-a-half years and as old as seven years. The decision for a child to move from one classroom to another should be based on the observable developmental needs of the child, not chronological age.

The concept of the three-year age span is based on (you guessed it!) observable behaviors of children. As a botanist friend of mine advised on newly planted perennials: "First year sleep. Second year creep. Third year leap." Children grow in much the same way.

First year sleep

The first year in a Montessori classroom doesn't seem to bring any huge change in the child. The three-year-old seems happy, content, and busy, creating independence and concentration though activities more focused on the practical skills of self-care and care of the environment, indoors and out.

Second year creep

The second-year student, the four-year-old, becomes interested in learning how to write his or her name, counting numbers, and doing other academically oriented work. Vocabulary becomes impressive. The four-year-old begins a period of rapid physical growth. The legs become longer, and some of the baby-like features of the three-year-old disappear.

Third year leap

It is the five-year-old, the third year student, who seems to burst into learning. Reading and writing work explodes. Math work, with all four operations, using materials with numbers up to 9,999 is commonplace. The five-year-old experiences a year of mastery with the growth of the first two years coming to fruition.

Sleep. Creep. Leap.

Challenges for the three-year age span

Outside forces can challenge the structure of a primary Montessori classroom and the vibrancy the three-year age span creates. Five-year-olds may leave to go to public kindergarten, leaving the three-year structure diminished.

In some states, the mandated adult-to-children ratio for childcare facilities changes from one to twelve for three-year-olds to one to twenty for five-year-olds. Many schools feel financial pressure to create "kindergarten" classrooms to take advantage of this more relaxed ratio. There may also be pressure from parents to show that the school has a separate kindergarten program and is not just a preschool. If a five-year-old is reading, parents may insist that school administration move their five-year-old up to *elementary*, thinking the primary classroom doesn't have anything to offer a five-year-old reader, when in fact the primary classroom offers appropriate learning opportunities that can accommodate academic work through at least the third grade level. More importantly, the primary environment supports the overall development, not just academic work, of the child in this first stage of development.

> **Third year students assume responsibility for the well-being of their group.**

These factors—five-year-olds leaving, financial pressure, and parent requests for early elementary—can weaken or water down the vibrant environment that Dr. Montessori envisioned for the three-to-six-year-old. Removing a five-year-old from a primary classroom does not serve the best interests of the child, the classroom, and, in the long run, the school and the child's family.

Five- and six-year-olds in a Montessori classroom are able to use and develop leadership skills that they may not have a chance to gain elsewhere for many years. Amazing as it may sound, the third year students in a Montessori primary classroom assume many responsibilities for the well-being of their group. They eagerly help younger students with learning to put on shoes and coats. They organize lunch and clean-up routines, as well as read out loud to younger students. I've observed the changing of the guard during the last few weeks of school as the third year students instruct the second year students on how to do certain duties.

Whenever possible, commit your family to a full, three-year cycle of child development in a Montessori school. Encourage school administration to create clear guidelines and expectations for the school's families to safeguard a three-year-cycle for your child and all the children in your school.

Concentration and Independence

The pedagogical principles of the Montessori method are designed to help each child attain a strong level of concentration and to help him or her be able to "do it myself."

Concentration can be developed in two basic ways:

1. Doing a purposeful activity multiple times in succession, or
2. Doing a variety of activities over a longer and longer period.

The freedom in the Montessori classroom permits both of these methods to occur by allowing the child to choose activities that are meaningful to him or her.

The basic rules of the classroom aid the development of concentration. These simple rules follow:

1. Choose your own work.
2. Work at a table or rug.
3. Do not touch someone else's work.
4. Put your work away, ready for the next person, when you are finished.

If we could get everybody in the world to follow those rules, world peace might have a chance!

Once a child has chosen an activity, he or she has the freedom to work on that activity for as long as he or she would like. Since self-mastery is a need of the child, the Montessori teacher protects the child from being interrupted by other children and

> *Self-mastery is a need of the young child.*

from being required to "share" the materials of the activity the child seeks to master.

The materials in a Montessori classroom are self-correcting in some form or another. For example, the Pink Tower is self-correcting with the child's visual sense and the laws of physics. If the ten blocks aren't placed in proper order, the tower doesn't look quite right, or it will fall over. Read more about the Pink Tower on page 54.

Glassware is used extensively for practical life lessons. Careless movements cause breakage. Broken dishes help children self-correct movement in a way that plastic or wooden items cannot.

An interesting observation about the glassware in a primary Montessori classroom: most of the time only one or two items are broken each year. When a vase or glass breaks, the entire class seems to "self-correct" from the incident. Once children become aware of the consequences of their movements, they tend to become more in the moment and engaged in their activities, thereby developing greater and greater concentration. Careful movement contributes to concentration. Concentration leads to learning.

Them that has china plates themselves is the most careful not to break the china plates of others.
J.M. Barrie

Independence is developed with the child's cycle of work in a Montessori classroom. Choosing work and dealing with the consequences of those work choices fosters independence. The child learns to trust his or her judgment by making choices and working through the challenges of those decisions.

In a Montessori classroom, the child uses breakable dishes, uses knives and potato peelers, carries expensive wooden boxes

The right to do work contains a corresponding factor of responsibility.

and maps, and pours buckets of water. The child is shown how to use these items in a safe and careful manner and learns that the right to do certain work contains a corresponding factor of *responsibility*.

The child is also shown how to self-correct when an object is dropped. For example, each child is given a lesson on how to clean up spilled water and sweep up spilled beans or rice.

These lessons also reinforce grace and courtesy by showing how to ask for assistance in cleaning up broken items or, how to offer help when a lesson tray scatters.

Each Montessori environment is prepared, physically and socially, in such a way as to aid each child in his or her acquisition of concentration and independence.

Free Choice

When we allow free choice, we give the child the freedom to select the work he or she finds meaningful.

Dr. Montessori asked us to have faith in the child's ability to self-construct. This gift of faith is what we need to give to our children. Seeing our children happily working in a prepared environment with clear structure and expectations, we should be able to have faith in the child's abilities.

As parents and adults, we are eager to see our child develop. We encourage the first step, the first word, the first of everything. Encouragement can lead to pushiness, though, and then to unconscious demands on the child.

A Montessori trainer told the story of a four-year-old girl coming into the classroom, free choice at risk of being lost. "Mommy told me to work with the Moveable Alphabet this morning," the girl told her teacher while shaking hands as a morning greeting. The Moveable Alphabet is a box of loose letters used for spelling and writing.

"Sweetheart," her teacher answered. "We'll let your mommy come in to do Moveable Alphabet if she likes. What's important is what would *you* like to do this morning?"

There are times that we might have to entice children to join us in lessons in areas they might avoid, which is more about removing obstacles to development than limiting free choice. This leads us to our next concept, *freedom within limits*.

The idea of *free choice* is discussed in more detail in *Chapter 8, Assuring Success.*

She (the directress) understands and believes that the children must be free to choose their own occupations just as they must never be interrupted in their spontaneous activities. No work may be imposed—no threats, no rewards, no punishments.

Maria Montessori

The Absorbent Mind, page 240

Freedom within Limits

The ideas of freedom within limits and freedom linked to responsibility are concepts that people sometimes have difficulty understanding. The freedoms in a Montessori classroom are to be safeguarded by the adults in charge. It is the freedom within limits of responsibility that create the essential dynamic of a Montessori classroom.

Children in Montessori classrooms aren't free to do anything they like, but as mentioned with E. M. Standing's story in the previous chapter, children do know that "we like what we do."

To the outside observer, it may appear the children are allowed to do anything they like. Sometimes parents become disgruntled because their child isn't allowed to do a certain lesson or to do somersaults across the classroom. These parents are under the misperception that children in a Montessori classroom are allowed to do anything they like.

What we should see when we observe a classroom are children who "like what they do."

One of the reasons they like what they do is that they understand the limits of their freedom. As I used to tell my students, "You are not here to roll around on the floor, run around the classroom, or be loud and rowdy with your friends. We are all here to work, learn, and have fun. The freedom you have is with your choice of work."

Children intuitively understand the truth and power in those words.

In a few short weeks, children new to the classroom respond to the gift of a prepared Montessori environment and use free choice and freedom within limits to truly choose what they do and do what they choose.

> **Free choice allows the child to select meaningful work.**

Read more on freedom in *Chapter 8, Assuring Success.*

Understanding Creativity, Imagination, and Fantasy

Montessori principles work because of an understanding of the nature of fantasy in the child, the origins of creativity, and the work of the imagination.

From birth to six years of age, the child is a literal learner. One could say that the child is learning the facts of life. This is red. This is blue. This is a duck. This is a goose. Facts are of enormous interest to the young child.

As in the old computer adage, "garbage in, garbage out," the child in the first plane of development requires a diet of correct information, based on reality. The young child's needs and interests lie more in the stories of what happened that day to people he or she knows instead of fairy tales such as *Snow White and the Seven Dwarfs.* When the child enters the second plane of development, around age six to seven, fairy tales, which offer moral development and excite the imagination, will appeal to the child.

Children under the age of six are enthralled with true life stories such as *What I Bought at the Grocery Store* and *What I Saw as I Drove to Work.*

For the young child in the primary Montessori classroom, we offer sensory and language experiences that help develop the intellect. With *sensorial materials,* we give the experience and precise language for concepts such as temperature, height, length, volume, weight, color, shape, form, geography, sounds, tastes, and much more.

> There is nothing in the intellect which was not first in the senses, but it exists in the intellect in a different mode from in the senses.
> Aristotle

So what does this all have to do with creativity, imagination, and fantasy?

Imagination, in the young child, is not yet well developed. To fully utilize its power, the imagination depends on a mind filled with correct information. How can we imagine the landscape of the South Pole if we don't have correct sensorial information and language about cold, ice, water, islands, continents, mountains, and oceans? The child in a Montessori primary classroom is given these sensorial and language experiences to use later as the power of imagination fully develops in the elementary years and beyond.

Creativity is the ability to bring an idea into existence. An idea forms in the imagination. Through skill and knowledge, the idea is realized, whether it is a thought or a skyscraper. The ability to imagine and create depends on having a rich supply of sensorial information and language already absorbed by the intellect.

Perhaps an example of children having a tea party can illustrate the use of imagination and creativity. Let's say a couple of four-year-olds decide to have a tea party. They imagine having a tea party. To create the tea party, they begin by setting the table. For many children, that is where the ability to create ends as they do not have the skill or imagination to bring real food and tea to the table. At that point, the food at a tea party becomes imaginary or a creation of fantasy. Fantasy takes over where skill and understanding end.

Fantasy is a creation of the imagination that exists only as thought. It can't be realized on the physical plane. Young children accept fantasy as literal fact. This can be difficult to change.

Justin was a four-year-old who was having night terrors. He cried to his parents about being kidnapped by evil monsters, and the only person Justin thought could protect and save him was Spiderman. There was no convincing Justin that his big, green, toothy monsters did not exist or that Spiderman was a comic book character. Justin insisted to his parents that he needed Spiderman to come and protect him. After a week of sleepless nights for the entire family, Justin's parents decided that they would have to fight Justin's fantasies with "real" fantasy.

Justin's dad came home with a gift for Justin, a piece of netting from "Spiderman" and a signed "Spidey" note with instructions to hang the net across Justin's bedroom door at night. The gift did the trick. Justin, and rest of the family, slept all night under the protection of your friendly neighborhood Spiderman. A fairy tale ending for a case of fantasy run wild.

Fairy tales are loved by the child not because the imagery he finds in them conforms to what goes on within him, but because these stories always result in a happy outcome, which the child cannot imagine on his own.

Bruno Bettleheim

The information collected by the intellect is used by the imagination to create. Montessori work gives children reality-based information, knowledge, and skills children can use to develop productive imaginations.

This work of the intellect—using correct information to imagine and then create—leads us to another important Montessori concept, the work of the hand and the mind.

The Work of the Hand and the Mind

Having a prepared environment full of meaningful hands-on activities that engage the child's intellect is another reason Montessori education works. We might say that the child's hands working with the *Montessori materials* helps the child's brain grow in effective ways. The nerve connections between the hands and the sensory cortex in the brain account for almost a fourth of all sensory inputs in the entire body.

As the child works with the prepared lessons in the Montessori classroom, he or she begins to create with the hand a mental construct of certain qualities and relationships in the world.

On the next page we'll talk about one of the most recognizable pieces of work in a Montessori classroom, the Pink Tower, featured on the cover of this book. The child's work with the Pink Tower, as with all Montessori materials, creates a foundational experience that reaches across the entire Montessori educational continuum, from childhood to adolescence.

> **A child's hands working with the Montessori materials helps the child's brain grow in powerful ways.**

The human hand, so delicate and so complicated, not only allows the mind to reveal itself but it enables the whole human being to enter into special relationships with its environment. We might even say that man "takes possession of his environment with his hands."

Maria Montessori

The Secret of Childhood, page 81

The Pink Tower

"When will my son stop playing with the blocks in the classroom and start to do some real work?" This is a question I've heard many times from concerned parents. Parents are anxious to see some tangible results of their child's time in the classroom. I can think of no better learning pastime than "playing" with the blocks in a Montessori classroom. Let me show you the Pink Tower.

In the Montessori primary class (for three- to six-year-olds), we introduce the Pink Tower to the three-year-old as part of the sensorial work to help develop visual discrimination. The Pink Tower stands prominently in the classroom, ten pink-colored cubes. The largest, the ten cube, is ten centimeters on each side and the smallest, the one cube, is a one-centimeter cube. Dr. Montessori took the butcher's wooden weighing blocks and painted them pink to make a tower enticing to the child.

With the Pink Tower, the child works on a rug and carries one block at a time with both hands. It takes ten trips over and ten trips back to get all the blocks to the rug, so this activity builds concentration and memory.

The work with the Pink Tower also is a lesson in physics with the child's inner teacher asking some of these questions: What combinations of blocks can I stack and the tower will continue to stand? What other building combinations can I make besides a tower? What relationships does the Pink Tower have with other materials in the classroom? The physics of the work is the child's exploration.

The Montessori teacher doesn't pose these questions to the child. It is the child's mind that poses the questions, consciously or unconsciously, as the child explores and discovers the answers on his or her own by manipulation of the materials over a period of time in the primary classroom. As the child works with the Pink Tower, the child's body and mind absorb information that will help in future math work. At the simplest level, the Pink Tower is a set of pink building blocks. As the child explores the other materials of the Montessori classroom, the child will begin to see relationships within this material and among other materials.

For example, the child will discover that the ten-cube is much heavier than the one-cube. Perhaps in counting the Thousand Chain, a Montessori material of beads grouped by tens to a thousand, or working with the Golden Bead Material used to build numbers concretely up to 9,999, the child will make the connection that the ten-cube is one thousand times heavier than the one-cube; that its numerical value is one thousand times greater than the one-cube; and that its volume is one thousand times greater.

Numerical value is not an abstract concept in the primary Montessori classroom. Working with the Pink Tower helps the child know by sight and feel the difference between one and a thousand.

Many children enjoy drawing the Pink Tower. The Pink Tower lends itself to artwork and challenges the child to figure out how to draw a cube, how to maintain the proportion of the tower, how to shade, and more.

For the six or seven-year-old elementary student, we "borrow" the Pink Tower from primary to make the initial presentation for the Cubing Material, a set of cubes and prisms that allows children to explore algebra in a hands-on manner. We introduce the idea that each cube of the Pink Tower has a mathematical name and numerical value. The smallest cube is represented by 1^3 and the ten cube is written 10^3.

With the Cubing Material, the elementary student uses the algebraic binomial, $(a+b)^3$, and trinomial, $(a+b+c)^3$, formulas in a concrete way. With the Cubing Material children can transform the cube of one number to another cube by adding prisms and smaller cubes. The children's explorations lead them to analyze and name the parts of the new cube and derive the algebraic formula for the cube built with two values, a+b. The eight pieces of this binomial cube, $(a+b)^3$, can each be given a mathematical name. This can also be done with the twenty-seven parts of the trinomial cube, $(a+b+c)^3$.

Binomial Formula:

$$(a+b)^3 = a^3+3(a^2b)+3(ab^2)+b^3$$

Trinomial Formula:

$$(a+b+c)^3=a^3+3(a^2b)+3(a^2c)+b^3+3(ab^2)+3(b^2c)+c^3+3(ac^2)+3(bc^2)+6(abc)$$

We allow children to use their imagination (usually in their sixth elementary year *if* they are interested) to use these keys and derive the quadranomial formula, $(a+b+c+d)^3$, on their own.

For the older child who has a desire for more mathematics, we will revisit the Pink Tower in the form of the Cubing Material to derive the cube root of numbers to ten million.

For geometry work in the elementary, the child can derive the formulas for volume and surface area from the cubes of the Pink Tower. Geometric progression is an inherent concept within the Pink Tower. With primary and elementary students, we can further explore the Pink Tower by rolling and moving the cubes through a tub of sand or flour, thus creating a footprint of a solid moving through space and a concrete, hands-on experience with ideas from calculus.

The beauty of the Pink Tower, and all the other Montessori materials, is that there are multiple physical concepts embedded in the materials, whether we are cognizant of them or not. Children and adults, and amazingly even Montessori teachers, do not need to be aware of the concepts of numerical value, weight, geometry, art, engineering, or calculus to enjoy working with and learning from the materials.

As in the Zen proverb, "When the student is ready, the teacher will appear," the Montessori analog could be, "When the student is ready, the concept will appear."

When your child tells you he or she worked with the Pink Tower today, you can say with sincerity, "I'm glad to hear you are doing such important work."

The child only deeply understands that which he has created.
Jean Piaget

CHAPTER SUMMARY

The Montessori method works because it is based on observing the activities of each child within a well-defined learning environment.

Within the Montessori environment, children engage in activities of their choice during a three-hour work cycle. A trained adult observes and assists as appropriate. It is the child's self-directed and purposeful activity that leads to greater independence, concentration and rapid personal growth.

With a typical traditional educational curriculum, one size must fit all. Such a curriculum is based more on the needs of adults than the needs of children.

Success in a Montessori program is determined by the understanding and implementation of the following principles:
- Four Planes of Development
- Human Tendencies
- Pedagogical, or Teaching and Learning, Principles
- Prepared Environment
- Three-Hour Work Cycle
- Three-Year Age Span
- Concentration and Independence
- Free Choice
- Freedom within Limits
- Understanding Imagination, Creativity, and Fantasy
- The Work of the Hand and the Mind

The prepared learning environment of a Montessori classroom includes materials, such as the Pink Tower, that contain multiple physical concepts that children explore by using the hands and the mind together.

Chapter 3

Montessori Principles: More than Teaching

Teaching as Part of Human Development

In Chapter 2 we talked about the four stages of development, sensitive periods, and human tendencies. Montessori pedagogical principles are based primarily on these three concepts.

What we'll discuss in this chapter are basic tenets of child development and how Montessori principles., methods and techniques are incorporated into Montessori learning environments. This chapter should not be construed as a substitute for Montessori teacher training, but instead should be viewed as a method of helping you, the parent, see your child in the larger picture of human development.

Developing Trust and Respect through Teaching

The young child asks us to "help me help myself." Our children are born with a vibrant urge to become independent and capable. Montessori education is designed to help children help themselves by developing independence and concentration.

Our children are strangers in a strange land. They need our help and assistance to learn how to make their way in the world.

To help us with that goal, we need to consider the specific developmental needs of children, wherever they are on the developmental continuum. Let's look at the developmental needs of young children.

The child is truly a miraculous being, and this should be felt deeply by the educator.

Maria Montessori

The Absorbent Mind, page 121

Developmental Needs of the Child from Birth to Six Years

From your child's birth through his or her sixth year, your child learns in a way that is very different from the way he or she will learn after this period of time. Your child is in sensitive periods of growth for the development of language, movement, social relations, sensory refinement, and a sense of order.

We absorb information from our culture, and our development unfolds in a predictable pattern and timetable no matter where we live in the world. During the first two years of life, learning to walk and talk appears effortless. Under normal circumstances, nobody has to teach a human being to speak or how to walk. We, as well as parents all over the world, impatiently wait for our child's first word and then wonder if our three-year-old will ever stop talking.

During the first six years of life, human beings acquire 90 percent of our daily spoken vocabulary. We learn a multitude of physical skills. We develop family relationships that form the basis of a lifetime of relationships. We learn to identify tens of thousands of sounds, smells, tastes, sights, and physical sensations. We begin to order and classify our world in a multitude of ways, from vegetable, animal, mineral; living or non-living; edible and non-edible; yummy or yucky; hot and cold; good or bad; and on and on.

Sensitive Periods, Birth through Six Years:

Language

Movement

Order

Refining the Senses

Social Relationships

When we are aware of our children's learning sensitivities at this age, we can be of great service to their development by providing opportunities for these learning proclivities to be utilized.

Sensitive Periods Guide Learning

With these powerful learning sensitivities, our children learn how to interact with the people in their world. These sensitivities, guiding the acquisition of language, movement, sensory development, order, and social skills, all come into play in how our children see the world and the part they will eventually play in the world.

It is during their preschool years that our children unconsciously learn the fundamental skills that will take them through life.

The Learning Needs of the Older Child: Ages Six to Twelve Years

As your child loses his or her first tooth and begins to cut adult teeth, the brain's development also changes, and learning becomes more conscious and adult-like as the young child's learning sensitivities fade away. Between the ages of six to twelve years, the child's learning style is now characterized by a mind that wants to reason things out. "Why do we need to shake someone's hand when we meet them?" a six-year-old will question. A four-year-old, on the other hand, learns to shake hands as a fact of life and focuses on the how of a skill and not the why.

This age child desires to break away from the familiar circle of home. This is when you will start to get requests to spend the night at friends' homes. You'll

> **Learning Needs of the Older Child:**
>
> *Use of Imagination*
> *Use of Reasoning Mind*
> *Working in Groups*
> *Sense of Morality*
> *Joining Society*

see that this age child prefers to work and play in a group versus doing activities alone. The older child's learning is fueled by the imagination and not so much by absorbing the environment as with the younger child. The elementary-aged child possesses a developing sense of morality, and learning comes from the desire to understand right and wrong, good and evil, justice and injustice.

Montessori Principles Create an Action Plan

Montessori principles create an action plan that utilizes your young child's developmental strengths. The older child, as mentioned, has very different needs and strengths. The older child, though, will meet with more success when the skills learned before the age of six are strong and positive.

The young child has other learning strengths that the older child does not possess. The younger child loves repetition. You may have noticed this in your child. This age child loves to have the same book read over and over, sing the same songs, and watch the same movies. Young children learn from doing the same thing over and over and over again. Older children and adults get bored by repetition and require seeing the same material in different and interesting variations, or as we say in Montessori terms, they require "repetition with variety" to learn.

The younger child has a love of order and likes to know that things are going to be the same. The young child thrives on knowing that meals will be served at anticipated intervals; that materials for play and work activities are in a predictable place; and that there is a familiar routine and rhythm to each day and week.

The young child thrives when using his or her hands to learn.

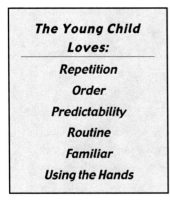

The Young Child Loves:

Repetition

Order

Predictability

Routine

Familiar

Using the Hands

Neuropsychologists are beginning to understand how brain development and learning depend on children's use of their hands to interact with their environment, in conjunction with repetition, order, predictability, routine, and familiarity.

It is in the family that the child becomes familiar with life's critical lessons. It shouldn't surprise us that family and familiar come from the same root word.

Montessori principles use your young child's sensitive periods and learning style to develop foundational skills that will enhance growth and learning immediately as well as in the elementary years and all of life.

Montessori Lessons Work

After more than twenty-five years of working with children, I know there are specific teaching principles and techniques that help children learn in rich and satisfying ways.

Montessori lessons clarify to your child how life is lived in his or her community and in our culture. Lessons based on Montessori principles aid your child's development toward independence and concentration, the actual goals of learning. Each of the lessons a Montessori teacher uses is based on tried and true teaching and learning principles. Let's look at some of these principles.

Tried and True Teaching Principles

As to methods there may be a million and then some, but principles are few. The man who grasps principles can successfully select his own methods. The man who tries methods, ignoring principles, is sure to have trouble.

Ralph Waldo Emerson

Emerson saw that if we understood principles we'd be able to devise successful methods for whatever set of circumstances in which we found ourselves. If we focus only on methods, we risk missing the forest because of the trees.

Our methods should be based on principles. Here are some of the teaching principles on which Montessori methods are based.

Respect

The most important teaching tool that we need is respect for the child. We cannot demand respect from the child; we can only give it. The paradox of life is that when we give respect, we get it in return.

As we work with our children, we must give them the utmost respect as they are involved in the crucial work of constructing a new human being, a being unique to this time and place.

Living my teenage years in Germany and going to German school gave me an insight into the young child's world and work. Trying to learn a new language, the rules of conduct, the turn of a phrase, the use of an idiom, using my fork with my left hand, and sampling new foods were at times overwhelming.

How I appreciated the kind soul who patiently pointed out the socially acceptable way to eat, behave, and express myself. How much more I learned eating dinner with my German tutor's family than I ever learned from a teacher yelling at me about what I was doing or wasn't doing. *Vielen Dank, Frau Kowohl.*

Being in a new culture helped put me in a position to understand the dilemma of a young child. The young child is intelligent and eager to learn but often misunderstood and viewed as not smart enough or not old enough to do something. When you are in a new culture, natives may dismiss you as not being capable or comprehending when, in fact, the situation is more about the ability to express yourself in an unfamiliar language and experience.

> *If our actions are ruled by love and respect for the child, we can usually recover our fumble.*

The young child is in a new culture that he or she is trying to learn. We need to understand and respect children as they have new experiences and learn to express themselves and their needs.

Working with children, we will make mistakes and do things that we wish we hadn't. If our actions are ruled by love and respect for the child, we can usually recover our fumble.

Respect is the most important principle in the bag of teaching tools. We need to be sure that it is always the first one we select.

Awareness of sensitive periods of the young child

As we have previously discussed, the young child is in critical areas of development for language, movement, order, refinement of sensory skills, and social relationships.

Supposing I said there was a planet without schools or teacher, where study was unknown, and yet the inhabitants—doing nothing but live and walk about—came to know all things, to carry in their minds the whole of learning; would you think I was romancing? Well, just this, which seems so fanciful as to be nothing but the invention of a fertile imagination, is a reality. It is the child's way of learning.

Maria Montessori

The Absorbent Mind, page 24

Use knowledge of human tendencies

When working with the child, Montessorians keep in mind that human beings naturally tend towards behaviors that involve activity, becoming, belonging, exploring, orienting, order, communication, imagination, exactness, repetition, and perfection.

Prepared environment

When we can prepare the child's environment in such a way as to aid in their life and development, we make for happy and healthier children. We'll have details on the prepared environment in the next chapter.

Limitation of materials

In a Montessori classroom, we don't have one of every piece of material for each child. Usually there is only one piece of each material per classroom. For example, there is usually only one Pink Tower in a classroom. In our homes we need to structure the amount of activities for our children, thinking about how that activity is or is not aiding our child's physical, mental, emotional, and social/spiritual growth. Learning to wait and sharing classroom materials helps children develop impulse control and alternative thinking.

Teacher as link to the child and the world

As parents and teachers, we are in a unique position to connect our children to the world around them, first in our homes and also in our larger communities. In many ways, we are like magicians explaining a trick to a rapt audience. We need to keep foremost in our minds that the adult is the most important part of a child's environment.

Freedom of choice

When we are given a choice to do something or not, or a choice between one activity or another, we bring to our work (and play) an enthusiasm that might have been extinguished under force. When we give our children choices, we are helping them become good decision makers, and we help them bring a powerful force of will to their learning. For more about freedom of choice, see *Chapter 8, Assuring Success.*

Development of responsibility

As we learn new skills, we work our way into more freedoms and their corresponding responsibilities. The child's learning to peel and slice a banana might naturally lead to a freedom to eat a banana whenever the child desires. The responsibility coming from this freedom is to eat what you take and to clean up after yourself. The development of our children's skills leads directly to a freedom and its corresponding responsibilities in a kind of upward spiral: activity followed by skills, followed by freedom, followed by responsibilities, followed by new activity, and on and on.

The child is constructing a human being

Children are constructing the adults they will become. We might say, "The child is the father of the man." In each child is a powerful will that responds to the opportunities within the child's environment. We need to provide opportunities for the child's *self-construction* and remove obstacles to the child's development.

Start with the big picture, then go to the parts

When working with our children, we need to show them the big picture and then show them the parts. For example, our children understand so much better the answer to "Where do I live?" if we start with the planet Earth first instead of giving our street address.

We might say: Where do you live? You live on the planet Earth that is going around the sun once a year. It is spinning on its axis once a day to give us day and night. The Earth is covered by water and land. We live on the land. The land is formed into masses called continents. We live on the continent called North America, in a country called the United States of America, in the state called Oregon, in the county called Multnomah, in the city called Portland, on a street named Quimby.

Go from the concrete to the abstract

Add a globe to the previous explanation of where you live and you will make your talk more understandable to your child. Using a globe makes the discussion less abstract and more concrete. Whatever concept we can help our children hold in their hands, the clearer their understanding will be.

A six-year-old student of mine had a habit of making unkind remarks. My teaching assistant brought in a tube of toothpaste and asked this student to squeeze out some toothpaste into a small bowl. "Now put it back into the tube, please."

"But it won't go back in. Once it is out, you can't put it back in."

"Ah," my assistant said, "sort of like the unkind things you say to your friends."

By going from the concrete to the abstract, my student finally understood how her words couldn't be taken back, even with an apology.

The mind develops through the work of the hand

The hand and the mind work together in unexplainable ways. Try to thread a needle and your tongue comes out, as if your brain was trying to make a word to describe the experience. Children remember the names of objects better when they are able to touch or hold the object versus just seeing the object or a picture of the object.

Whenever we can involve the hands in a child's activities, we should. Neuropsychologists see that using the hands is children's most important learning advantage and that the work of the hand may be the most critical aspect of brain development and learning. Montessori classrooms are full of hands-on materials and methods to take advantage of each child's time-sensitive learning opportunities.

Isolate the difficulty in the task

Our words and our motions can seem to be a rushing river of sound and activity to our children. Listening to a language in which I'm not fluent reminds me of how language can sound to the young child--too fast to understand. But if the speaker talks slowly and perhaps hands me an object and names it, my comprehension soars. Watching a gymnast do a routine in the Olympics can appear to be breathtakingly complicated. When we get to see the routine done in slow motion or view a few steps in isolation from the entire routine and perhaps try the movement ourselves, the action becomes clearer.

To the young child, many of our adult words and actions can seem like a gymnastic routine in a foreign language. In our Montessori lessons, we isolate the difficulty of when to say or do something and show precisely how to do that thing.

Non-interference of spontaneous activity

Once a child chooses an activity, the teacher's job becomes one of not interrupting the child's initial and fragile focus. Her motto might be, "Don't just do something. Stand there."

In Dr. Montessori's words, "The great principle which brings success to the teacher is this: *as soon as concentration has begun, act as if a child does not exist.*" (*The Absorbent Mind*, page 255)

Observe the child at work

By watching our children when they are involved in an activity we will gain important clues into their skills, their need for new skill-building activities, and their personalities. Observing our children lets us know who they really are.

There is only one basis for observation: the children must be able to express themselves and thus reveal those needs and attitudes which would otherwise remain hidden or repressed in an environment that did not permit them to act spontaneously. An observer obviously needs something to observe, and if he must be trained to be able to see and recognize objective truth, he must have at his disposal children placed in such an environment that they can manifest their natural traits.

Maria Montessori

The Discovery of the Child, page 48

Repetition through variety

Human beings learn through repetition. The young child learns through repeating the same activity sometimes hundreds of times a day. The older child and adult need repetition but with some change in the activity, providing a new challenge. For the younger child, our challenge is to provide opportunities for repetition by keeping activities in an anticipated order and by allowing the child adequate time to repeat an activity as many times as necessary. When we give a lesson, we need to make sure we give our children sufficient time to do the activity multiple times.

Indirect preparation

Every time I think of indirect preparation, the movie *The Karate Kid* comes to mind. "Wax on. Wax off," Mr. Miyagi, the karate instructor, tells the Karate Kid as he polishes Mr. Miyagi's car.

Seemingly wasting valuable instruction time on waxing his teacher's car frustrates the Karate Kid. Once in the karate lesson though, a big grin breaks across his face as the Kid realizes that the strokes used to wax the car are the same ones needed for a difficult blocking move. And he does it effortlessly.

With our lessons, we want to prepare our children with activities that will strengthen their skills needed for later and more difficult work. Wax on. Wax off.

Techniques that lead to the child's mental and physical independence

Our ultimate job as parents is to raise an adult. We are raising adults, not children. Any unnecessary help we give to our children is a hindrance to their development. When we can help our children think for themselves and do for themselves, we can feel confident that we are doing our jobs as parents and teachers.

Concentration and independence—that's what we are looking for in the work of the child.

Next we'll look at some of the teaching methods that Montessori teachers use to implement principles.

Teaching Techniques

And so we discovered that education is not something which the teacher does, but that it is a natural process which develops spontaneously in the human being. It is not acquired by listening to words, but in virtue of experiences in which the child acts on his environment. The teacher's task is not to talk, but to prepare and arrange a series of motives for cultural activity in a special environment for the child.

Maria Montessori
The Absorbent Mind, page 7

Fostering mental and physical independence

Now that we have discussed the teaching principles that are inherent in Montessori based lessons, let's look at some of the techniques used to help foster your child's mental and physical independence.

Inviting the child

Each time that Montessori teachers want to show a child a new skill-building activity, they begin by inviting the child to the lesson. There are various ways to invite a child. For many of the children in my classroom, I'd only have to smile at them and they knew I had something new and fun for them to do. Other times children would come to me and say they needed a lesson on one thing or another. Other children needed some type of enticement to come to a lesson.

A child should always have the opportunity of saying "no" to an offer of a lesson. A teacher should graciously let it go and try again later that day or the next day using indirect preparation, another teaching principle.

Waiting for the teachable moment

When you observe your child doing various activities, you will notice that there is a step that needs refining or a further challenge that needs to be introduced. It is tempting to barge in while your child is in the middle of an activity and correct the situation. Don't. Invite the child to a lesson at another time and show the skill again with an emphasis on necessary information.

For example, perhaps your child is using too much soap from the pump dispenser when washing his or her hands. Present a hand-washing lesson giving interest to the amount of soap used. Make a point. "Just this much soap." This also isolates the difficulty your child is having with the soap.

Indirect preparation

Indirect preparation is both a teaching principle and a technique as shown by Mr. Miyagi in *The Karate Kid*.

If your child is having trouble using a spoon, then preparing different spooning activities with various materials, sizes of spoons, and amounts to spoon from one bowl to another can indirectly improve your child's dinnertime skills.

Observing the child

Not every child needs every lesson. It is through our observations of children that we know what to teach, when to teach it, when to repeat the lesson, and when to stop the lesson. As mentioned previously, observation of the child involved in meaningful activity is a Montessori teacher's most important activity.

Non-verbal techniques

Silence is golden for learning to the young child. Words and movements can get easily out of sequence and become quite confusing for the child.

I've given many presentations by saying only one word: "Watch."

We teach to the right hemisphere first in the young child. More on right/left brain workings under *Show, Don't Tell* on page 75.

Experience before language

Our children understand better (and I think adults do too, but I have no research to prove it) when we give them the experience before the language.

When I try a new dish at a restaurant, I like to taste it without really knowing what is in it. As I taste it, I try to figure out the ingredients. For some reason, the experience is more vivid for me if I don't know the name of the dish or the recipe. I want the experience of tasting the new dish before the language, not language before or during the experience. Experience, then language.

Point of interest

The concept of a point of interest allows us to present a lesson multiple times but in a fresh manner highlighting an action more clearly. To use hand washing again: for points of interest we could use the amount of soap used, the amount of water, the removal of suds, the amount of time spent washing, drying the hands, putting on lotion, making sure the sink is left clean, the counter is dry, the floor is dry, the child's clothes are dry, and many more. With our point of interest, we can highlight that next step on which the child needs to focus and give the same lesson multiple times with a fresh perspective.

Accessibility to materials

If we give a lesson and then make it inaccessible to the child, we have set up an obstacle to the child's development of mental and physical independence. Once we show a child how to do something, we need to make sure that the materials to do that activity are easily available to the child. Of course, there may be situations that make it necessary for safety's sake to keep certain materials out of reach.

Three-period lesson

The three-period lesson is an important Montessori teaching tool. It is used to introduce new words or concepts by introducing three items at a time. Two items may offer inadequate challenge, and four can be confusing. The three-period lesson goes like this:

First Period: Introduction

This is a circle. This is a square. This is a triangle.

(Note: These are wooden puzzle figures from the Geometric Cabinet.)

Second Period: Show Me

Show me the triangle. Show me the square. Show me the circle.

We do many repetitions with the second period of the lesson, using a variety of expressions, such as: Please put the circle in my hand. Place the triangle on the table. Carry the square to the chair.

Third Period: The Test

Point to the object and ask: What is this?

If the child can name the item, add another object. If not, return to the second period of the lesson.

Sometimes all three periods can be done in one session. Other times, it may be weeks between the first and third periods of the lesson with many repetitions of the first and second periods.

Show large contrasts first

When introducing new material, Montessori teachers strive to introduce three items with great contrast, such as in the above example of introducing a circle, a square, and a triangle.

As the child's discernment grows, lessons to introduce and learn the shape and names for circle, oval, and ellipse are given. These similar curvilinear figures would not be the first lesson on shapes because we would want to show figures with the greatest contrasts first.

Control of error

In each lesson there is an element that makes the work self-correcting in some manner. This may be the material itself. It may be the child's visual or aesthetic sense. To use the Pink Tower example, if the child places one of the blocks out of sequence, the tower may topple. The law of physics is the control of error. There are some combinations of putting together the Pink Tower that will work and not be in its usual graduated sequence. The child's memory and sense of order act also as a control of error.

The Essence of a Montessori Presentation

We've talked about the teaching principles and techniques behind these lessons. Let's look at how to give a presentation and consider how the presentation works.

Lessons are short

Many of the initial presentations given to the three- and four-year-old are for the most part one to five minutes in length. The Montessori teacher invites a child to a presentation, gives the presentation, and then goes on to other matters at hand.

Don't worry about doing the same thing over and over

Since the young child learns through repetition, your child will love to see and do the same activities literally hundreds of times. Preschoolers can sing "Rudolph the Red Nosed Reindeer" 365 days a year with enthusiasm. In my primary classroom, I knew if I asked what songs the children wanted to sing, Rudolph would always be on top. The young child asks for you to read *Good Night Moon* every night for years. When I sat down to read to my preschoolers, mentally I was always prepared to read the same book at least three times through. Your child can repeat the same prayer every dinner and never become bored with it. It becomes the familiarity of family.

Around the age of six years, this love of repetition will fade away, and children will begin to respond to familiar activities with "I'm bored" and "That's boring." Until that moment, Montessori teachers are prepared to repeat and repeat and repeat.

Be patient, it will come

One of the frustrations with teaching young children, as parent or teacher, is that we never know when a child will grasp a concept. It could be the first time we show something. It could be the ten thousandth time. During those long periods, there may be a temptation to say, "How many times have I shown you how to…?"

We show. We explain. We model. In the back of our minds, we may think, "Every other child does it, so…what is your problem?"

This is when respect needs to come out of the teaching tool bag. A child may learn something with the initial presentation or with the one-hundred-ninetieth lesson. Each time, though, we need to come to the presentation with profound respect for the child's immense task of building a human being.

When we are at wit's end thinking, "How many times do I have to show you about flushing the toilet?" remember this: We'll have to present the lesson a few more times. We need to ask ourselves also if we have been showing enough and not just telling.

Show, don't tell

Presentations to the young child should be short and sweet. Lessons should also use as few words as necessary. Remember, experience before language. Otherwise the actions of a task get tangled up in the words, and the job becomes confusing for the child. Taking in instruction visually is a right brain function, and taking instruction verbally is a left brain function.

For the young child, one might think of lessons as introducing a concept to one hemisphere at a time. The first presentation is for the visual right brain. Later, talking about the lesson connects to the left hemisphere or verbal part of the brain. This teaching technique makes learning easier for children. It is the child's free-choice repetition of the activity and expressive vocabulary that help create neural pathways between the hemispheres.

Give the experience first, language later

When someone tries to show me how to do something and explains it as they go, I can get terribly confused as the presenter pushes buttons and talks at the same time.

For example: *Highlight your word. Click on this icon.* Screen changes. *Scroll down to font. Double click.* Screen changes. *Click on subscript. Click on okay.* Screen changes. *Then click on the body of the letter.* Screen changes. *There you are.*

It easier for me to learn if you give me written words as instructions and let me figure out the motions by myself, or if you slowly show me the sequence of actions and let me write down the instructions as you go. Give me a chance to do it a few times on my own and ask questions if I need help. Give me words and actions all at the same time, and I won't learn a thing.

The young child is the same way. Montessori teaching techniques take that into account.

Teach to the periphery

A child may refuse to come to a lesson because the child is scared or shy. Montessori teachers teach to what I call the "periphery." For the child who is too timid to join me in a lesson, I'll give the lesson to another child in earshot or view of the child who needs the lesson. Children learn out of the corner of their eyes, too. Once trust is established, children usually come happily to a lesson when invited.

Be prepared

When you watch a Montessori teacher in action, his or her actions may appear effortless and easy to duplicate. My experience is that it takes many repetitions to feel comfortable with the motions of a lesson. Montessori teachers have learned hundreds of developmentally appropriate activities, have practiced them literally for hundreds of hours, and have been tested to certify that they are proficient in their understanding and utilization of each lesson.

I know teachers who have taught for twenty years who still practice an hour or two a week on refining their lesson techniques.

A sample lesson

On the next page is a sample lesson from one of my Montessori teaching *albums* describing how to present a practical life skill, using a spoon. Then we'll look at some more teaching techniques.

USING A SPOON

Prerequisite: Child can sort and transfer objects with fingers

Materials Needed: Two bowls, a tray, a child-sized spoon, uncooked dry beans.

Presentation:

- Place two bowls on tray. Fill one bowl half full with dried beans. Place spoon on tray.
- Place tray on child's activity shelf. Invite child to lesson. "I'd like to show you a spooning lesson."
- Carry tray with both hands to the table. Place the tray on the table so that the bowl with the beans is on your subdominant side. If you are right-handed, your right hand is your dominant hand and your left is your subdominant hand.
- Pick up the spoon with your dominant hand and scoop up a spoonful of beans.
- Keeping the spoon level, transfer the beans to the other bowl. When the spoon is over the center of the other bowl, lower it slowly into the bowl and tip it slightly so that the beans fall into the bowl.
- Repeat this process until all of the beans have been transferred.
- Turn the tray around so that the full bowl is on your subdominant side.
- Invite child to spoon the beans. When the child is finished, help the child return the tray to the activity shelf.

Purpose of Lesson: Coordination, order, concentration, and independence.

Control of Error: Spilling the beans, leaving beans in the bowl.

Points of Interest: Getting all the beans transferred, turning the tray, holding the spoon level.

Language: Spoon, material being spooned.

Age for presentation: 2½ to 6 years.

Later work: Using different size spoons, bowls, and materials.

> To become acquainted with the material, a teacher should not just look at it, study it in a book, or learn its use through the explanations of another. Rather, she must exercise herself with it for a long time, trying in this way to evaluate through her own experience the difficulties of, or the interests inherent in, each piece of material that can be given to a child, trying to interpret, although imperfectly, the impressions which a child himself can get from it. Moreover, if a teacher has enough patience to repeat an exercise as often as a child, she can measure in herself the energy and endurance possessed by a child of a determined age. For this final purpose, the teacher can grade the materials and thus judge the capacity of a child for a certain kind of activity at a given stage of his development.
>
> Maria Montessori
> *Discovery of the Child*, pages 152-153

Count to ten between steps

In presentations, Montessori teachers go slowly and use only essential movements. This necessitates practicing the presentation many times before giving it to a child in order for the exercise to appear clear and precise. Many times when giving a presentation I mentally count to ten between steps in order to assure that I am going slowly enough for the child to fully absorb the experience.

Say "thank you"

Montessori teachers usually thank each child after a presentation by saying something as simple as, "Thank you for coming to my lesson."

Lessons in a Montessori classroom are by invitation. Lessons have slow and deliberate motions and contain as few words as necessary. Lessons are respectful of the child and are as short as possible. A "thank you" communicates a lot of respect to the child.

Teach, don't correct

After the child begins to repeat an activity, Montessori teachers understand that this is not the right time to correct. Montessori teachers help with a difficulty only if a child asks. The teacher makes note of where in the activity the child has difficulty and presents the lesson again on another day, giving special emphasis or making that step "a point of interest" as we say in Montessori teaching terms.

A teacher may offer to help a child but does so mainly in the context of the Golden Rule. If a child drops a lesson and pieces are all over the classroom, the teacher, as well as other children, may ask if they may help pick up, respecting the child's right to refuse assistance.

Not every child needs every lesson

No teaching book could cover all the learning situations that a child will encounter. It also follows that not every child needs every lesson. With observation, a Montessori teacher zeroes in on the pertinent lessons for each child. For example, if we observe a child tying his or her own shoes correctly, we don't give a lesson in shoe tying.

Relight the candle

Patience is another important teaching tool. An amazing and frustrating thing about the young child's learning is that ability comes and goes. The child will learn something and then forget it. The candle blows out. We have to relight the candle by teaching that skill again. We teach and teach until, at some point in time, the skill is firmly embedded in memory.

These fluctuations in learning are due to the developing brain's formation. Until neural pathways in the brain are well trod, instruction and memory may not be easily retrievable by the child.

When you begin to work with young children, you may not have a lot of patience. By the time your child turns six, you'll probably have a lot.

Going from the known to the unknown

Through observing the child at work, the Montessori teacher uses what the child knows to show him or her the next step in learning. For example, a Montessori teacher will make sure that a child has a firm understanding of the three basic geometric shapes of square, circle and triangle before introducing one at a time the materials for rectangle, trapezoid, rhombus, oval, ellipse, quatrefoil, scalene triangle, isosceles triangle, and equilateral triangle.

Be friendly with error

We learn more from our mistakes than from our successes, and in a Montessori classroom, the teacher is friendly with error. The dropped lesson, the spilt pitcher of water, the materials left out, and the broken flower vase are all handled in a matter-of-fact and friendly manner. What we see when we are friendly with error is the child's energy and enthusiasm for tackling new challenges and finding fresh and creative ways of doing things.

A new student to my elementary classroom, Raj, hadn't had a lesson in the Box of Sticks, a plane geometry material that uses colored sticks of ten varying lengths. These sticks can be clipped together to form polygons and angles or can be tacked to a corkboard to illustrate various concepts in plane geometry. As I read a chapter out loud to the class, Raj took the lesson materials from the shelf and began to place sticks and tacks on the board.

I wasn't happy that Raj had taken the materials from the shelf without a lesson and had taken advantage of my reading to the class to help himself when he should have asked for a presentation first. As soon as I finished the chapter, I walked over, probably more like marched if the truth were known, and asked Raj what he was doing.

Raj looked up at me with big, brown, puppy dog eyes. "I'm writing a song."

"Hmm. A song with the Box of Sticks." I squinted to avoid rolling my eyes in disbelief.

"See, Ms. Maren. This red stick is middle C. You can play it on the Tone Bars or the Bells with me."

Off we went. Following Raj's stick instructions, I played the first two lines of Beethoven's "Ode to Joy."

If I hadn't been reading, I would have been "unfriendly" and stopped this process of using one type of material to do something fresh and creative. Raj is the only student I ever had who used the Box of Sticks to write a song. Nurturing enthusiasm for learning is only one reason we need to be friendly with error.

Instilling confidence, promoting creativity, learning to take calculated risks, viewing our work as valuable and feeling a sense of purpose also flourish when we provide an atmosphere that is congenial towards mistakes and experimentation.

Assure success

For many years, I spent at least a week per year observing in schools other than my own. I tried to do a variety of schools, public, parochial, Montessori, as well as different grade levels.

As I was having lunch in a school's teacher's lounge, I listened as a fifth grade teacher ranted about one of her difficult-to-work-with students. "I'm hoping he flunks this test so I can fail him. I want him to fail. He deserves to flunk."

Coming from my Montessori perspective, I was speechless at this teacher's remarks and horrified that a teacher could have an attitude like that about her student. Then I remembered one of my college professor's words: "I am here to teach, and you are here to learn. My job is to teach. Yours is to learn. My job is to teach, and if you learn in the process, that's all good and fine. Your learning is *not* my job or my problem."

Montessori philosophy is such that we assure the child's success by teaching in ways that assist the child's learning. We observe to make sure a child learns. If the child isn't learning, then we observe for obstacles and work to remove those obstacles. No child deserves to fail. No child deserves a teacher who thinks so.

Montessori teaching techniques assure your child's success in learning, which is much more than teaching. Your child's learning *is* a Montessori teacher's job.

Ready. Set. Let's go.

Respect. Patience. Understanding the sensitive periods and developmental needs of children under six. Using tried and true teaching principles and techniques. The Montessori teacher teaches in order to help your child learn and be successful in his or her choice of activities. It's what children need.

In the next chapter, we'll look at how a Montessori

environment works and show the connections between teacher, child and the Montessori prepared environment.

In brief, the teacher's principle duty in the school may be described as follows: She should explain the use of the material. She is the main connecting link between the material, that is the objects, and the child. This is a simple, modest duty, and yet it is much more delicate than that found in the older schools, where the material simply helps the children understand the mind of the teacher, who must pass on her own ideas to a child, who must in turn receive them.

Maria Montessori

Discovery of the Child, page 151

CHAPTER SUMMARY

Children have unique developmental needs from birth to around six years of age called sensitive periods. These sensitive periods for learning include the acquisition of language, movement, order, sensory refinement, and social relationships.

Children between the ages of six and twelve years have different needs. The elementary aged child learns through use of the imagination, use of the reasoning mind, a desire to work in groups instead of individually, use of a developing sense of morality, and a requirement to get out into the larger world.

Montessori education applies proven developmental principles using concise teaching techniques that engage children's learning in powerful ways. Each lesson given is based on time-tested and scientifically deduced methods, techniques and materials.

Syd Kruse

Chapter 4

How Does a Montessori Environment Work?

Understanding the Magic of Montessori Education

In *The Secret of Childhood*, Dr. Montessori wrote, "The most striking response, and one that is almost like a magic wand for opening the gate to the normal expression of a child's natural gifts, is activity concentrated on some task that requires movement of the hands guided by the intellect."

What happens in a Montessori classroom to create this "striking response that is almost like a magic wand?"

If we were lucky, we attended a school where we felt engaged, respected, and were able to express and use our natural gifts. But for many of us, we find the joy and absorption that people say they see children experience in a Montessori classroom difficult to imagine.

Maria Montessori, through observation of children, developed materials that engage both the hands and the mind of the child. Science and research, especially in the past twenty years, have come to prove that Montessori's observations accurately describe the learning needs of children and have shown as well that the principles Dr. Montessori envisioned do create joyful learners.

Steve Hughes, a pediatric neuropsychologist and Assistant Professor for Pediatrics and Neurology at the University of

Minnesota Medical School, says it quite simply: Montessori students are "good at doing things." Dr. Hughes has reported that 75 percent of his fellow pediatric neuropsychologists have children who attend or have attended Montessori schools, mainly because what happens in a Montessori classroom supports current knowledge on brain development. Dr. Hughes goes so far as to say: "It's like education designed by a gifted pediatric neuropsychologist!" For more information about Dr. Hughes and his views on Montessori education and current brain research, visit his website: GoodatDoingThings.com.

Perhaps the most scientific and rigorous research on the effects of Montessori education is that of Angeline Stoll Lillard. In 2006 Dr. Lillard examined students at Craig Montessori, a public school in an urban, minority neighborhood of Milwaukee, Wisconsin. The study used other Milwaukee students and schools as a control group. Dr. Lillard found that "Montessori children performed significantly better" in both

> *"It's like education designed by a gifted pediatric neuropsychologist!"*
> *Dr. Steven Hughes*

cognitive/academic and social/behavior dimensions. These findings were true for both the 5-year-old and the 12-year-old study groups. For more information on Dr. Lillard's important research see her book, *Montessori: The Science Behind the Genius* and her article "The Early Years: Evaluating Montessori Education" in *Science* magazine, September 29, 2006.

Montessori graduates tell us they can and do make a difference in their families, in their schools, in their communities, and in their world. Montessori students agree that they are "good at doing things."

The most striking response, and one that is almost like a magic wand for opening the gate to the normal expression of a child's natural gifts, is activity concentrated on some task that requires movement of the hands guided by the intellect.

Maria Montessori

The Secret of Childhood, pages 137-138

As previously mentioned, successful Montessori classrooms and schools adhere to three major concepts that together create a powerful learning experience for children:

1. Prepared environments based on three-year age groups
2. Children's free choice of activity within a three-hour work cycle
3. Adults professionally trained in Montessori philosophy, methods and materials for the group they are teaching

A Montessori school is the physical environment for children, parents, families, and Montessori-trained adults to come together to establish a *community* dedicated to the work of the child. This dedication creates more than a classroom or a school. This coming together of adults and children builds a Montessori community.

The Prepared Environment

There are four basic prepared learning environments, each designed for distinct developmental needs as your child matures.

1. Infant-Toddler: from birth to three years
2. Primary: from three to six years
3. Elementary: from six to twelve years
4. Adolescent: from twelve to eighteen years

The primary program was established first, with the first school beginning in 1907 in Rome. Today, the most available environments in Montessori schools are the primary and elementary programs. Infant-toddler and adolescent programs require different resources and are not as commonly found but are rapidly growing in popularity. A description of each learning environment follows.

Why does your child need a prepared environment?

Each Montessori learning environment provides your child a place for his or her own age-appropriate work, a place to develop as a unique person, a place to gain a wider experience, and a place to manage him or herself independently. These environments allow your child to learn confidence and experience a dignity children seldom find in our adult-centered world.

The environment itself is moreover something special. Though it is provided by adults, it is in reality an active and vital response to the new patterns manifested in the life of a growing child.
Maria Montessori
The Secret of Childhood, page 140

All over the globe, Montessori communities, regardless of socioeconomic or cultural factors, have discovered the power of Dr. Montessori's faith in a child's ability to self-construct, or to create a unique human being, through free choice activities in a prepared environment.

A Montessori prepared environment is designed to meet, at any age, your child's request of "help me help myself."

Let's look now at the four types of Montessori prepared environments.

Infant-Toddler Communities: From Birth to Three Years

The greatness of the human personality begins at the hour of birth.
Maria Montessori
The Absorbent Mind, page 4

Supporting families from the beginning

Montessori infant-toddler programs are referred to as their own communities, and Montessori-trained adults guide parents and babies in becoming families. Adults who are trained in creating and fostering infant-toddler communities are called Assistants to Infancy.

Schools that offer infant-toddler programs may offer one or more of the following options:

Prenatal Classes
Parent and Infant Class
The Nido
The Young Children's Community

Prenatal classes

Prenatal classes help parents understand the parents' nurturing role during pregnancy. An Assistant to Infancy presents your child's developmental turning points and psychological and sensory perspectives.

Sometimes very small children in a proper environment develop a skill and exactness in their work that can only surprise us.
Maria Montessori
The Secret of Childhood, page 87

Parent and infant classes

Parent and infant classes allow you to learn with your child under the guidance of a trained adult using an environment prepared especially for children and parents.

Observation of your child is encouraged in order for parents and caregivers to offer appropriate activities to the child. Typically these classes meet for two hours, twice a week. Class size is usually ten parent/child combinations with two trained staff members.

The Nido: from two to fourteen months

The needs of your child at this age include a need for movement, a need for language development, a need for independence, a need for love and security, a need for leadership (discipline), and a need for order. These continue until around age three.

The environment of the *Nido*, or "nest" in Italian, is equipped with materials designed to meet your baby's developmental needs. The Nido contains customized stands, stairs, and bars for your baby to use for movement. A quiet and isolated sleeping area is available for these infants. Babies gain independence with activities that aid movement. Child-sized tables are used for eating instead of high chairs, allowing a baby the dignity to move freely. A baby-to-adult ratio of three to one is recommended in the Nido.

When your child begins to walk, he or she enters into a new community, the infant or the young children's community.

The Young Children's Communities: from fourteen to thirty-six months

At approximately fourteen months, your child is comfortable walking and is ready for different challenges. The young children's community serves the needs of up to twelve children with two trained adults while focusing on the individual needs of each child.

A larger environment offers more options for motor development and contact with nature for your child. There are three distinct areas in this environment: movement, practical life, and language

Movement

The space for the community includes special areas for your child's movement that allow for work with stairs and pushcarts as well as materials to help develop hand-eye coordination. Individual work focuses on movements, such as "back and forth" and "in and out." Children at this age hold a fascination for a movement until it has been mastered then move to a new activity. For example, once opening and closing a drawer is perfected, repetition stops, and the child's interest turns to another skill.

Practical Life

In the Practical Life area your child can prepare his or her own snack, clear the table, sweep, wash dishes, wash clothes, and care for plants and animals. These practical activities of everyday life allow your child to gain confidence in mastering simple chores while developing independence and concentration.

Language

The Language area provides for group and individual lessons with vocabulary cards, miniature objects, and books. Spoken language activities and other expressive skills such as art and music are also part of your child's environment.

Around age three, your child will have developed language, coordinated movement, and the ability to function independently. At this point, he or she will be ready for a new challenge, the primary environment.

Your child entering the primary class from the young children's community will exhibit a love of work, concentration on his or her activities, a level of self-discipline, and a joyfulness that a three-year-old who is new to Montessori works to attain.

Both my daughters, Dana and Hannah, joined a young children's community as they turned a year old. After Dana, the oldest, was in the classroom for a couple of weeks, I went to observe at lunchtime. As I stood in the observation room, I watched as she set her place for lunch with a placemat, napkin, and fork, poured a glass of water, carried it to her place for lunch, then sat down at her just-right-sized table. Dana sang a song, ate her lunch, and cleaned her place afterwards. Off she went to make up her pallet for nap. It was all quite cheerfully done.

That's the moment I first saw the magic wand that Dr. Montessori described. Twenty-seven years later I'm still amazed at "the normal expression of a child's natural gifts."

Primary Environments: From Three to Six Years

Building a foundation of independence and concentration

Your child enters the primary environment, or *Children's House,* during a development period critical for language, order, movement, social relations, and refinement of sensory perceptions.

The magic of this time involves the child's free choice to engage in activities in five basic areas: practical life, sensorial, language, mathematics, and cultural work. These distinctions are made for the adult mind. Your child perceives only fun and interesting activities.

As soon as children find something that interests them they lose their instability and learn to concentrate.

Maria Montessori

The Secret of Childhood, page 145

Practical Life

Practical Life work develops a wide variety of skills necessary for personal independence, from buttoning clothes, peeling carrots, sweeping the floor, watering plants, and arranging flowers, to name only a few. Practical life activities center around self-care, care of the indoor and outdoor classrooms, and lessons in grace and courtesy to others.

From these activities, your child will learn to choose his or her own work, how to define his or her workspace, how to self-correct, how to move about the classroom while carrying objects, and how to interact positively with other children in the classroom. Lessons of grace and courtesy help your child develop positive social skills. These accomplishments create a sense of well-being for all the children in your child's learning community.

Refinement of the senses

Sensorial activities use specially designed materials to help your child develop minute discriminations by sight, sound, touch, taste, and smell. Many of these materials are appealing wooden materials in various shapes and colors.

Work with the Pink Tower, explained in Chapter 2, helps the child with these experiences:

- Allows the child to visually differentiate 1/2 cm when stacking each cube.
- Creates a hands-on experience for geometric progression as the child touches the squares and cubes of numbers to ten.
- Allows the child to feel the weighted differences among the cubes, that is from one gram for the smallest cube increasing by the cube of the number to ten cubed or one thousand grams.

The Pink Tower work requires ten trips from the stand to the work mat, ten trips back, and a decision where each block must be precisely placed, thus aiding concentration and independent decision making.

Montessori-designed sensorial materials are *keys to the world* that allow your child to have hands-on, foundational experiences in language, math, geometry, reading and writing, living skills, cultural activities, and the five senses.

For example, the "key" to understanding the world of color begins with knowledge of the three primary colors, red, yellow, and blue—which are presented in the lesson with the First Color Box. The secondary colors and tertiary colors are presented in the Second Color Box and are also found in the set of colored pencils for the Metal Insets in your child's classroom. The Third Color Box allows your child to create a color wheel and explore the concepts of hues and shades of color.

So it goes for every activity in a Montessori environment. It may appear to the adult as simple playing, (or worse, boring repetition), but a myriad of direct and indirect objectives are quietly being assimilated by your child as hands and intellect work together.

Your child may choose to do an activity over and over, perhaps for days. This is the point where a trained observer needs to ask, "Is the child following an inherent need for repetition, exactness, and perfection? Is the child exploring and making new discoveries and connections about this material? Or is this child avoiding other activities because of fear or other issues?"

The trained Montessori teacher, guiding your child's activities, is a crucial element of the prepared environment. Your child's teacher is a child advocate who respects your child's total being and your role as your child's first and most important teacher.

Montessori teachers may be aided in the classroom by an *assistant* who acts as a paraprofessional.

Language

Language work in the Children's House begins with the Sandpaper Letters and the "I Spy" game. With this work, your child first learns the sound of each letter instead of the letter's name, along with the fine motor skills necessary to eventually draw each letter.

Exploration of the language materials gives your child the keys to learning any language as your child learns to write, then read, using the Sandpaper Letters and the Moveable Alphabet. As your child begins to read, the language area contains cards, booklets, and a beautiful miniature farm to aid your child's discovery of the function of words, or grammar, in our language.

Mathematics

Mathematics work for your child begins with the practical life and sensorial work. Working with these activities helps your child develop essential movements along with various visual and tactile discriminations that include length, height, width, quantity, area, volume, and shape. For more on the sensorial materials, see Chapter 10.

Children under the age of six perceive the length of an object to contain the mathematical value of the object. For example, children see one long object as "more" than three similar yet shorter objects.

Research shows that preschool children perceive the length of objects to be the indicator of quantity instead of the actual number of objects. Children were asked to say which of three vases contained the most number of flowers. One vase had three flowers. Another vase had five flowers. The third vase had two flowers which were about three inches taller than the flowers in the other vases. The children chose the vase with the two tall flowers as having the most flowers.

After a visit to Santa Claus, three-year-old Dana and her six-year-old cousin Bryan had identical candy canes. Dana's cane dropped and broke into three pieces.

"It's not fair. He has more than I do." There was no convincing Dana that Bryan had the same amount as she did. She wanted the long peppermint stick. To her, it was more. Bryan, in a different stage of development, traded his one long stick for the three short pieces. Peace again ruled the day.

Dr. Montessori, through observing children, understood that children in the first plane of development perceive value from the length of an object and not the number of objects. This is why your child's concrete math experiences begin with the Red Rods, ten rods whose lengths graduate from ten centimeters up to a meter. The Number Rods along with colored Bead Bars represent values from one to ten and are introduced after the sensorial experience of the Red Rods. The numerals for one to ten are introduced to your child in isolation from these concrete, hands-on materials as learning numerals requires a different skill set from discriminating length or quantity.

Mathematical magic occurs once your child connects the concepts of number values with symbols from one to ten. The key to exploring the decimal system is the knowledge of values to ten. Once this happens, your child will be ready to explore the Golden Bead Material and new mathematical concepts.

The Golden Bead Material, also known as the Decimal Material, introduces your child to units, ten, hundreds, and thousands. With this material your child learns to add, subtract, multiply, and divide quantities up to 9,999. The Golden Bead Material is limited to thousands in order for your child to discover the next group of numbers. Working with later materials such as the Stamp Game and the Small Bead Frame, your child discovers the next grouping, ten thousands.

Understanding the Golden Bead Material holds the key for comprehending any number system and numbers to infinity.

Cultural work

Cultural activities for your child include colorful wooden puzzle maps, flags, and indigenous articles from around the world. Your child will explore with pictures the peoples of the world and physical geography.

Other materials for cultural work may vary from classroom to classroom and country to country as each Montessori community communicates its sense of place and customs through the prepared environment. An example of this might be seen in the different ways that people around the world eat together. Having high tea may be a practical life skill in a Montessori classroom in England, whereas in the United States it would be viewed as cultural work.

Social skills

Social skills are modeled and taught in the lessons of grace and courtesy in a Montessori classroom. From the basics of saying please and thank you, to learning how to politely interrupt a conversation, how to ask for assistance, how to greet a guest, and many more, your child is introduced to foundational skills for a lifetime of healthy relationships.

In a Montessori school, your family helps create your child's unique community through sharing of stories, sharing of customs, and sharing of food. A Montessori community reflects both the attitudes and enthusiasm of each family along with school staff.

Your respect for others in the community, your sharing of ideas, and your commitment to the success of the community determine the culture of your child's school. Thus, each Montessori community reflects the dynamic values of its families, staff, and children.

Elementary Environments: From Six to Twelve Years

Sowing the seeds of culture

As your child loses baby teeth, earlier learning sensitivities diminish and behavior changes. Your elementary-aged child has a need for group work, usually preferring to be involved with friends, in contrast to the individual focus on activity and mastery that motivated children's activities in the primary environment.

This is the time of life when we begin to hear the child make comments such as, "That's boring," or "That's not fair." The child, who in the previous plane of development said please, thank you, and excuse me, now enters into an age of rudeness. Because, duh, there is an entire universe out there to explore, and we really shouldn't waste their time on the trivial.

Instead of repeating the same exercise, the elementary child now requires repetition through variation. Work must also use the imagination, involve a sense of humor, allow going outside of school to have new experiences, use logic and reasoning, and exercise the developing sense of right and wrong.

Elementary age children might refuse to wear the clothes in their closet, change their hairstyle, and even alter their names. My daughter, Hannah, was a perfect example of this change, and there was no doubt when she entered the second plane of development. Hannah refused to wear her favorite lavender outfits and black patent leather shoes and demanded that her long blonde hair be cut off above her ears. In her new red and blue rugby shirts and corduroy pants, she would only answer to the name of Luke, in honor of Luke Skywalker.

The elementary age child shakes life up. The human tendencies of imagination, becoming, and exploration head to the forefront of how the elementary aged child looks at the world, and beyond.

Dr. Montessori urged us to show the child the universe. From *To Educate the Human Potential*: "Since it has been seen to be necessary to give so much to the child, let us give him a vision of the whole universe. The universe is an imposing reality, and an answer to all questions."

In presenting this idea of the universe to your child, Dr. Montessori asked us to be storytellers of the truth for *cosmic education*. The elementary child's learning and exploration grows from lessons called the Five Great Stories:

The Beginning of the Universe
The Coming of Life on Earth
The Coming of Human Beings on Earth
The Story of Communication in Signs
The Story of Our Numerals

If the idea of the universe be presented to the child in the right way, it will do more for him than just arouse his interest, for it will create in him admiration and wonder, a feeling loftier than any interest and more satisfying. The child's mind then will no longer wander, but becomes fixed and can work. The knowledge he then acquires is organized and systematic; his intelligence becomes whole and complete because of the vision of the whole that has been presented to him, and his interest spreads to all, for all are linked and have their place in the universe on which the mind is centered.

Maria Montessori

To Educate the Human Potential, page 6

The Five Great Stories are designed to fuel children's imaginations. The story of The Beginning of the Universe brings to the child the idea the basic laws of physics, chemistry and thermodynamics through the use of science experiments and impressionistic charts. The story asks the children to think about how our world and our universe came to be.

The story of The Coming of Life on Earth brings to the children the idea that at one time life did not exist on Earth. The story asks, what events had to happen to prepare the Earth to become a planet that could support life?

The Story of Human Beings on Earth fuels the children's imagination with a time line of geological evidence. Food for thought is given with the idea that at one time there were no human beings on our planet. What happened? How have human beings changed over many thousands of years? What is the story of human beings?

At one time human beings did not know how to write. The Story of Communication in Signs brings to the children this idea and asks them to imagine how life would be with no written language. The Story of Our Numerals is similar to the story of writing and brings to the children the idea of the importance of the language of numbers.

The lessons and work of the child in the elementary class flow from these five stories, and are designed to help inspire awe and appreciation in the child for those who have come before us.

The avenues for study in the Montessori elementary classroom are limited only by the children's imaginations. Some of the areas of study follow: literature, languages, mathematics, geometry, algebra, physics, chemistry, biology, art, music, dance, movement, zoology, botany, geography, social studies, history, cooking/nutrition, engineering/building, and ecology.

As your child explores the elementary environment, he or she will discover areas of personal interest while making connections to these major fields of human study and endeavor.

Your child, with knowledge acquired in a Montessori primary

classroom, now builds on this foundation. For example, the cubes of the Pink Tower are transformed in a rainbow of colors as the Cubing Material. The Cubing Material, a color-coded set of cubes and square-based prisms, will guide the child's exploration of the algebraic formulas for the binomial and trinomial and will help the child determine the cube roots of numbers to ten million.

Your child's practical life skills honed in the primary environment aid his or her science experiments in the elementary classroom. Reading and writing skills become tools for research. The concept of a million is built on your child's primary experiences with thousands—a thousand thousands. Working with millions in the elementary classroom continues to utilize hands-on concrete materials, such as the Million Cube and the Multiplication Checkerboard.

Your child's learning of the primary years becomes direct preparation for new and exciting work in the elementary environment. The keys of the world so easily absorbed in the primary years now begin to unlock the knowledge of the universe for your child.

And the magic continues.

The laws governing the universe can be made interesting and wonderful to the child, more interesting even than things themselves, and he begins to ask: What am I? What is the task of man in this wonderful universe?

Maria Montessori

To Educate the Human Potential, page 6

Adolescent Environments: From Twelve to Eighteen Years

Creating the person in society

In the past few years, the success of Montessori communities has led to the establishment of Montessori environments for the adolescent in both rural and urban settings.

Dr. Montessori envisioned an *Erdkinder* (German for "child of the earth") farm environment to help the young teenager fulfill a developmental need to connect and form a society of his or her time and place.

Montessori adolescent programs for twelve- to fifteen-year-olds, and recently fifteen- to eighteen-year-olds, seek to provide experiences such as running a small business or farm. Creative expression is encouraged through a variety of events specific to each community, such as dinner theatre presentations, community service, and multi-week-long outdoor learning expeditions. These activities help your adolescent reinforce self-confidence and self-mastery as he or she explores new connections to society and a larger world.

The young teen needs opportunities for the following:

- To strengthen self-identity
- To develop the intellect through critical analysis and debate
- To build community within a peer setting
- To serve others
- To understand societal methods and norms
- To express new and powerful emotions
- To understand the ways of the natural world

The Montessori prepared environment takes into consideration these needs and offers opportunities for the adolescent to focus on belonging to a self-organized group of peers, classmates, teammates, and friends. The teen's need for adventure, personal challenge, and self-discovery are addressed as well as the need to argue, disagree, and oppose others, especially parents, teachers, and other authority figures. There are opportunities for working with the hands—growing plants, crafts, painting, sculpture, and playing music. Poetry reading and writing are encouraged at this time of life when we love poetry for its power of expression. The environment is designed to aid the adolescent's developing sense of caring and compassion.

The young teenager's great intellectual growth of the elementary years is now put to practical use in the work of the adolescent. A boat-building project, for example, may require geometric knowledge to calculate the theoretical speed of the vessel using the square root, a concept that was first introduced indirectly with the Pink Tower to the three-year-old.

Adolescent programs differ based on the cultural needs and resources of their communities. These Montessori programs are designed with the same principles as younger children—the prepared environment with well-trained teachers, the use of teaching and learning principles, methods, and materials that develop concentration and independence, along with knowledge of periods of human development and human needs or tendencies.

Montessori principles when consistently applied create the power in a Montessori learning environment at each developmental stage of your child's life, "like a magic wand for opening the gate to the normal expression of a child's natural gifts."

CHAPTER SUMMARY

Three Montessori methods create a powerful learning experience for children:
- A prepared environment of hands-on materials
- Activities designed to aid concentration and independence
- Adult understanding, observation, and guidance of developmental periods for social, physical, emotional, and intellectual development

The prepared environment of the child becomes more than a classroom or a school. It is a community of families and adults dedicated to the work of the child.

A Montessori environment allows a child to express his or her natural gifts by providing an environment full of activities that require movement of the hands guided by the mind.

Montessori prepared environments are designed for specific age groups based on observable needs and tendencies for that age of child.

Syd Kruse

Chapter 5

What? No Grades?

The Dilemma

"We've loved having Jeremy in Montessori school, but it's time for him to go to first grade at a real school."

This is a comment heard by Montessori school administrators and teachers every spring.

Jeremy may be a thoughtful and considerate six-year-old who is reading, has memorized his multiplication facts, and can name all fifty states and their capitols, but his parents don't see his Montessori school accomplishments as valid.

Why?

Because one of the more disconcerting aspects for parents about Montessori education is the absence of grades and homework. It's not how we were raised, and it's difficult to give up those standards of traditional schooling. As a parent, I, too, struggled with the idea of no grades.

I believe that understanding Montessori methods can help parents feel confident that their children are moving forward in a meaningful manner and that Montessori principles are working in a powerful way in their children's learning. This chapter gives details about meaningful assessment while emphasizing Montessori principles and teaching techniques.

Oh, and besides no grades, did I mention no homework?

The role of education is to interest the child profoundly in an external activity to which he will bring all his potential.

Maria Montessori

From Childhood to Adolescence, page 11

What Gets Measured Gets Managed

Peter Drucker, considered the foremost management thinker in the twentieth century, wrote, "What gets measured gets managed."

It is essential that what we measure about our children's progress and development are qualities that are meaningful and important.

When parents are asked what they consider the most important items for their children to learn in life, parents answer with the following types of qualities:

- To have the ability to enjoy life;
- To value themselves;
- To be risk takers;
- To be self reliant;
- To be free from stress and anxiety;
- To have loving, peaceful lives;
- To celebrate their present moments;
- To experience a lifetime of wellness;
- To be creative; and
- To fulfill their higher needs and to feel a sense of purpose.

This list comes from Wayne Dyer's book, *What Do You Really Want For Your Children?* For almost twenty years, I've posed this same question to parents and have found these answers to be comprehensive.

What do most schools measure?

Results on standardized tests. Academic subjects such as reading, writing, and arithmetic that are measured and given letter grades.

But are we measuring what is important?

In 2008 the Pew Center on the States reported that in the United States, one adult in a hundred is incarcerated. The National Center for Educational Statistics reported with the 2003 National Assessment of Adult Literacy that thirty million adults have below basic literacy skills, with an additional sixty-three million adults having only basic literacy.

May I suggest that as a society we are not measuring what is important?

A major paradox of learning follows: academic achievement builds on the concentration and independence created through self-selected activities. When we focus on creating opportunities for meaningful work, high academics follow.

In the words of Frederick Herzberg, a psychologist who studied human motivation and achievement, "If you want people to do a good job, give them a good job to do."

In Montessori classrooms, we give children challenging work to do, and they rise to the challenge. Montessori programs choose to not give grades because these measurements do not reflect the development of the qualities that we should be looking for in children.

> *Are we measuring what is important?*

I believe the purpose of education is to help a child find his or her passion in life. Once passion is discovered, then an immense power is released, creating growth and learning.

Montessori teachers focus on guiding individual development by looking at a child's concentration on tasks and the level of independence the child shows in self-selected activities. In a child's personally chosen activities, we see the glimmerings of interest and passion.

In Montessori classrooms, our main purpose is not for our students to achieve stellar grades or high standardized test scores. We are striving to create opportunities for meaningful work from engaged people who are genuinely enthusiastic about their activities.

Paradoxically, high achievement follows.

Built-In Assessment System

Authentic Montessori programs have a built-in assessment system. Our real life experience, in whatever walk of life we follow, shows us that it is a short step of faith to know this: *The work is the test.*

Can you ride a horse?

Can you cook a meal?

Do you know enough math to balance your checkbook?

In our Montessori prepared environments, the child's work is the test. It is such a simple concept that we tend to overlook its brilliance. If you can do it, you know how to do it. That's real life testing. It's on-the-job training.

Why do we need grades and standardized tests to tell us what we should already know by observation?

The key element of a Montessori prepared environment is the trained adult observing the child at work. The adult guidance in a Montessori classroom is based on observations of each child. The lessons given are based on observation of individual children as well as the observations of the entire classroom in the context of overall development.

> **The child's work is the test in Montessori environments.**

We don't need to poke and prod to see what a child knows. We don't need to pull up the plant to check the roots to see if it's growing. We simply observe.

Authentic Montessori programs with trained adults provide the most effective assessment of the learning needs, as well as the accomplishments, of the child. This information, unfortunately, cannot be communicated as easily as using five letters of the alphabet or percentile rankings from a standardized test.

Remember, authentic Montessori programs have three key elements:

1. Adults professionally trained in Montessori philosophy, methods and materials for the group they are teaching

2. Prepared environments based on three-year age groups

3. Children's free choice of activity within a three-hour work cycle.

Montessori teachers' observations of children at work give insight into the development of each child. These observations consider any obstacles a child might be encountering in his or her development as well as the strengths, interests, and natural talents the child may express.

My vision of the future is no longer of people taking exams and proceeding on that certification from the secondary school to the university, but of individuals passing from one stage of independence to a higher, by means of their own activity, through their own effort of will, which constitutes the inner evolution of the individual.

Maria Montessori

From Childhood to Adolescence, Preface

The power of the guided observation skills of the Montessori teacher coupled with a Montessori prepared environment connects the child with purposeful activities.

Guided Observational Skills

My experience of trying to make sure my daughters, and later the children in my classroom, were performing at grade level has shown me the power of observation and guiding the child through the lessons in the Montessori prepared environment.

As I became conversant with public school standards and a variety of standardized tests, I realized that because of my observations and close working relationships with the children, I knew the grade level of each child for every subject without using a standardized test. The standardized test results for the children in my elementary classroom only confirmed the private knowledge that I had gleaned through observation.

There will be more about measuring academic growth later in this chapter.

My basic frustration with standardized tests was that the tests didn't touch on many academic skills the children in my elementary classroom possessed, concepts like finding square roots, working with exponential numbers, geometric concepts, United States and world geography, grammar, foreign language, scientific concepts, and more. For most of my fifth and sixth grade students, their math and language skills exceeded the eighth grade limit on the standardized tests.

As I became familiar with public school standards and standardized test levels, I realized the effectiveness of the children's work in the prepared environment to create powerful learning, much of which could not be communicated in the form of grades, grade levels, or national percentile rankings.

> *Without grades or external motivation, children create meaningful projects and challenging goals.*

I noticed that without grades or any external motivation, the children in my classroom created projects and challenging goals that I would never have assigned, much less figured out a meaningful letter grade.

An example

One of my third-year students started on a project to draw our state flag. The project grew to include drawings of all the state flags. Once that was completed, she added state birds, state flowers, and state mottos to each of the fifty flag pages she had created. The drawings in the project were beautifully drawn and colored. She then added a fact sheet for each state. This was a huge project for an eight-year-old, but it was one she developed on her own with determination, independence, self-motivation, and confidence.

What meaningful letter grade could I give that project? A++++++? What bubbles on what page do you color with a number two pencil to show those qualities of character?

Yes, the work is the test. We have to prepare the environment, stand back, observe, then prepare and observe some more.

> If you want people to do a good job, give them a good job to do.
> Frederick Herzberg

The Montessori Prepared Environment

Montessori classrooms, or prepared environments, as we discussed in Chapters 2 and 4, are designed for a three-year age span, except for the first three years of life.

For each of these age groups, a specific environment is prepared. Each classroom environment contains materials and lessons that have been time-tested (some over a hundred years) with children from all socioeconomic levels around the world. We know these lessons engage the children's personalities and give the children "a good job to do."

The successful workings of a Montessori classroom are based on the observations of the children at work. The work of the adult in a Montessori prepared environment is to observe and meet the developmental needs of each child. The prepared environment is specially designed to observe the child.

Each prepared environment contains the materials for hundreds of lessons and activities. Montessori prepared environments are dynamic places in which children find and choose meaningful work, do it, and feel the satisfaction of a job well done.

> I guess the essence of life for me is finding something you enjoy doing that gives meaning to life, and then being in a situation where you can do it.
> Isaac Asimov

Obstacles to Development

Where the challenge lies, for teachers and parents, is when a child is not learning. In Montessori terms, we say the child has encountered an *obstacle* to development. Montessori teachers, or *guides*, use their observations to direct the child over, around, under, or through developmental obstacles. These obstructions may affect intellectual, emotional, physical, or social/spiritual learning.

Please note that the spiritual learning mentioned here relates to something other than religion. Some people might be more comfortable with the term social instead of spiritual.

- Intellectual development refers to perception and problem solving.
- Emotional development refers to the passionate engagement with life.
- Physical development refers to control and coordination of the body.
- Spiritual or social development of the child refers to reason and freewill.

Obstructions to these four aspects of development are not easily measured by grades or standardized tests, though a low test score or low grades may signal that there are obstacles to development.

The work is the test. When we look at the child's self-selected activities (work) in a systematic way in relation to a continuum of human development, the child's progress and obstacles become evident. Later on in this chapter, we'll consider the observations and development of two four-year-old girls, Sara and Lily.

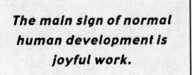

The main sign of normal human development is joyful work.

Four Indicators of Normal Human Development

What we have to keep foremost in our minds is what constitutes normal development. Dr. Montessori described characteristics of normal or natural development as signifying a process she called *normalization*. The four observable characteristics of natural development are these:

1. Love of work or activity
2. Concentration
3. Self-discipline
4. Sociability seen in joyful work, and cooperation

The main sign of normal human development at all ages is joyful work.

After twenty-five years of observing children at work, I believe that *these four attributes of normalization are what we should be assessing for all of our lives,* whether we are two or one-hundred-two. We are the person the universe intended when we are engaged in a task that makes us happy and brings happiness to others.

It is that simple. And it is that complicated.

Reflect on your own life. When one of these four attributes of normal development is missing in our lives, we know that we have run into an obstacle.

If we find we have trouble getting out of bed in the morning, we know our "love of work and activity" has met an obstacle.

When we find we can't "concentrate" on a task at hand, we know we've run into something that is keeping us from reaching our potential.

If we find we can't make ourselves do something we know that we should—losing ten pounds, writing thank you notes, or cleaning out the garage—we know that "self-discipline" has hit a snag.

When our work lacks "joyfulness"—we don't seek to help other people, or perhaps we go out of our way to make things difficult for others—our normal development is in turmoil.

Observing Obstacles

When we encounter obstacles to development, three basic behaviors can be observed. Dr. Montessori refers to these as *deviations* from normal development.

- **Eddying Out.** Our life seems to be stuck in the same place with no forward movement like a leaf caught in an eddy.
- **Detouring.** Our life heads in a different direction, which may or may not be beneficial for us.
- **Fighting the Rapids.** Our life feels like we are caught in the rapids of a river headed for the waterfall. We feel out of control, and the ride is bumpy and dangerous.

(For more about obstacles see Montessori's *The Secret of Childhood*, pages 154-173, and *The Absorbent Mind*, Chapters 12, 18, and 19.) Later we'll discuss what we need to do when we see the child struggling with obstacles.

Look for the Four Signs of Normal Development

As parents and teachers, we should first and foremost look for the four signs of normal development. If we see all four, we have little to worry about.

Well, that's all good and fine you say. But when your neighbor or sister's children come home from school with straight A's and your child gets a "normal development" report, how is that really going to make you feel? Doesn't quite sound like honor roll or college material, does it?

All of us want tangible proof that life is going well. Money in the bank. Hay in the barn. Groceries in the fridge. We crave confirmation that we have a future. We desire evidence of positive growth that we can share with family and friends.

Evidence is what we crave. We'll have the proof we desire when we understand these concepts:

- The work is the test
- The signs of natural and normal development
- The indicators of obstacles to development

Case Studies: Lily and Sara

Let's consider the observations of a couple of four-year-old girls, Lily and Sara. Lily is progressing at this time with no obstructions to her normal development. Sara, we'll see, is having some difficulties.

Montessori teacher trainers recommend that teachers keep observation charts or *activity charts* on their students. It is suggested that a teacher observe two students for a week at a time. The teacher continues to observe the entire class as well as give lessons, but the observation of the two students is intensive.

During the course of the thirty-six-week school year in a classroom of twenty-four to thirty students, each student would have at least three weekly activity charts that reflect the child's chosen activities as well as the levels of concentration and independence the child used. When I observed a child dealing with an obstacle to development, I included that child in each week's observations until the difficulty passed.

Here is a sample of an activity chart:

Activity Chart

Child Name: _____   Age: ____ *yrs* ____ *mos* Observer: _____

Date: _____	7:30	8:00	8:30	9:00	9:30	10:00	10:30	11:00	11:30
Deep Concentration									
Concentration									
Work, but Distracted									
Quiescence									
Slight Disorder									
Disorder									
Uncontrollable									

Comments: _____

_____

_____

Explanation of activity chart

The middle line is "the line of quiescence" which indicates that the child is at rest or is not engaged in an activity. As we go above the middle line, there are three lines that reflect the level of activity or work of the child.

- Work, but Distracted: Indicates that the child is involved with an activity, but other activities in the classroom distract attention.
- Concentration: Shows that the child rarely looks away from his or her activity.
- Deep Concentration: The child stays on task despite disturbances.

As we go below the line of quiescence, we see the following lines that represent levels of disorder in the child:

- Slight Disorder: The child has perhaps chosen work but

spends more time distracted than staying on task, or perhaps the child has not chosen work but walks aimlessly around the classroom and distracts others.

- Disorder: The child spends most of the time distracted or involved in activity that has no clear beginning, middle, or end.
- Uncontrollable: The child is involved in a tantrum, hurting other children, or angry outbursts.

Lily: On-course development

Let's look now at Lily's activity charts, keeping in mind the four indicators of normal development, signs of obstacles, and intellectual, physical, emotional, and social/spiritual development. For simplicity's sake, the worksheet on the next page contains three of the five daily charts of Lily's activities in her Montessori classroom.

As all of Lily's activities are above the line of quiescence, Lily displays strong concentration and independence in the classroom.

- Intellectually, the math and language work that Lily chooses over the course of this week shows that she is making challenging choices.
- Physically, Lily shows coordination through her activities of walking on the line and her ability to move through the classroom.
- Socially/Spiritually, Lily shows the four attributes of normalization, displaying calm and sociability in the classroom. Lily befriends others and shows sympathy and concern when a classmate skins her knee on the playground.
- Emotionally, Lily is able to verbalize that she is sad that her grandparents had to go home.

Lily displays all signs of normal development.

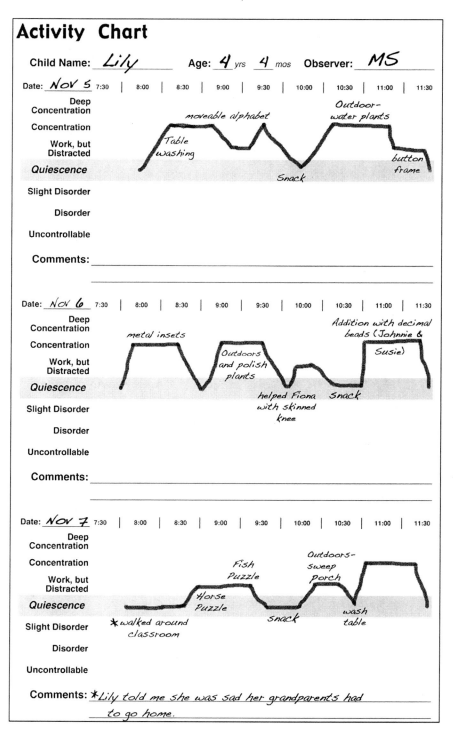

Activity Chart

Child Name: _Lily_ **Age:** **4** yrs **4** mos **Observer:** _MS_

Date: _NOV 5_ | 7:30 | 8:00 | 8:30 | 9:00 | 9:30 | 10:00 | 10:30 | 11:00 | 11:30

Deep Concentration
Concentration
Work, but Distracted
Quiescence
Slight Disorder
Disorder
Uncontrollable

moveable alphabet
Outdoor- water plants
Table washing
button frame
Snack

Comments: _____

_____

Date: _NOV 6_ | 7:30 | 8:00 | 8:30 | 9:00 | 9:30 | 10:00 | 10:30 | 11:00 | 11:30

Deep Concentration
Concentration
Work, but Distracted
Quiescence
Slight Disorder
Disorder
Uncontrollable

metal insets
Addition with decimal beads (Johnnie & Susie)
Outdoors and polish plants
helped Fiona with skinned knee
Snack

Comments: _____

_____

Date: _NOV 7_ | 7:30 | 8:00 | 8:30 | 9:00 | 9:30 | 10:00 | 10:30 | 11:00 | 11:30

Deep Concentration
Concentration
Work, but Distracted
Quiescence
Slight Disorder
Disorder
Uncontrollable

Fish Puzzle
Outdoors- sweep porch
Horse Puzzle
＊walked around classroom
snack
wash table

Comments: _＊Lily told me she was sad her grandparents had to go home._

115

Sara: Development meeting obstacles

Sara's activity charts on the next page indicate that Sara is dealing with a developmental obstacle.

Sara's concentration level is below the line of quiescence for the entire period. Checking Sara's charts, we see that Sara chooses the same work day after day and never attains a period of long concentration. We could say that Sara is "eddying out."

- Intellectually, Sara has met a developmental obstacle. Sara chooses work that is safe and not mentally challenging.
- Physically, Sara appears to be moving fine but dropped two lessons after bumping into a table.
- Socially/Spiritually, Sara seems to be withdrawing from group activities and is lacking the sociability that she has shown previously in the classroom.
- Emotionally, Sara has daily outbursts where she loses self-control.

When Sara's Montessori teacher visited with Sara's mother about what she had observed, Sara's mother confided that Sara's father and she were having marital problems. When Sara's parents saw the observable change in Sara's work habits and temperament, they understood the effect their quarrelling had on Sara and sought counseling. In a few weeks, as her parents' relationship improved, Sara's charts started to look like a child following normal development, charts more like Lily's.

> **Sara's Montessori teacher discovered a difficulty before it became a serious problem.**

Sara's Montessori teacher's observations discovered a difficulty before it became a serious problem—again, something that letter grades and standardized tests can't begin to describe.

Observation of the person involved in meaningful activity is our key assessment tool, not just in a Montessori classroom, but in all of life.

Activity Chart

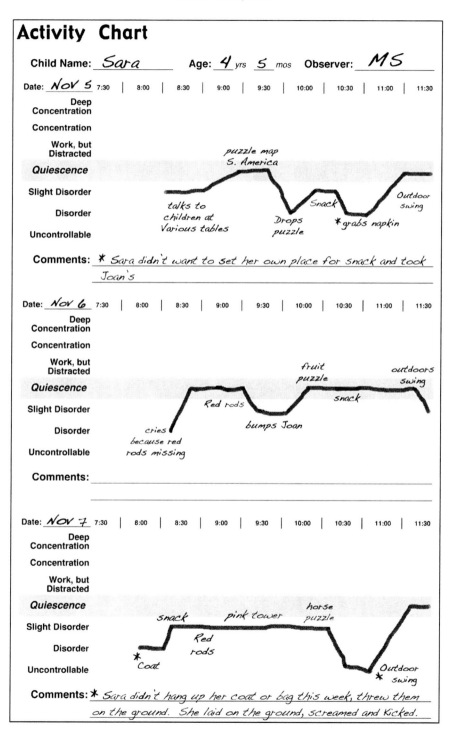

Child Name: Sara   **Age:** 4 yrs 5 mos   **Observer:** MS

Date: NOV 5   7:30 | 8:00 | 8:30 | 9:00 | 9:30 | 10:00 | 10:30 | 11:00 | 11:30

Deep Concentration
Concentration
Work, but Distracted
Quiescence
Slight Disorder
Disorder
Uncontrollable

puzzle map S. America

talks to children at Various tables

Drops puzzle

Snack

* grabs napkin

Outdoor swing

Comments: * Sara didn't want to set her own place for snack and took Joan's

Date: NOV 6   7:30 | 8:00 | 8:30 | 9:00 | 9:30 | 10:00 | 10:30 | 11:00 | 11:30

Deep Concentration
Concentration
Work, but Distracted
Quiescence
Slight Disorder
Disorder
Uncontrollable

fruit puzzle

outdoors swing

Red rods

snack

bumps Joan

cries because red rods missing

Comments:

Date: NOV 7   7:30 | 8:00 | 8:30 | 9:00 | 9:30 | 10:00 | 10:30 | 11:00 | 11:30

Deep Concentration
Concentration
Work, but Distracted
Quiescence
Slight Disorder
Disorder
Uncontrollable

horse puzzle

snack

pink tower

Red rods

* Coat

Outdoor * swing

Comments: * Sara didn't hang up her coat or bag this week, threw them on the ground. She laid on the ground, screamed and Kicked.

117

Observation Is the Key

When we see our children's activities stuck in an eddy, detouring off course, or out of control, we need to step back for deeper observation. We observe our children's behavior and try to understand the underlying need that is prompting that behavior. We try to discern our children's emotions. We ask questions and listen closely to what our children are telling us they need through their words and actions.

In our observations of Lily and Sara, we might say that Lily's behavior told us to give her more of the same. Sara's behavior, in contrast, communicated that Sara had needs that were not being met.

Behavior Is Need Driven

With observation of behavior we need to consider another important facet—the knowledge that human behavior is based on trying to fulfill needs.

Fundamental human needs can be defined in two ways: spiritual (or social) needs and physical needs. Below is a basic list of these needs. You may discover more than these.

Fundamental spiritual needs

- The need to belong includes: acceptance, appreciation, becoming, belonging, celebration, closeness, community, consideration, contribution, emotional safety, empathy, honesty, love, reassurance, respect, support, trust, understanding, and warmth.
- The need for activity includes: movement, exercise, creativity, exploration, and orientation.
- The need for communication includes: inspiration, laughter, fun, contemplation, and silence.
- The need for imagination includes: to choose dreams, goals, and values, create self worth, create meaning, create an authentic person, and create personal integrity.
- The need for order includes: beauty, harmony, peace, repetition, precision, and exactness.

Fundamental physical needs
- Physical needs include: air, food, light, movement, protection from danger, sleep, sexual expression, shelter, touch, and water.

Searching for Needs Behind the Behavior

As we observe behavior, we consider what needs are being met by the behavior. Whether the behavior is headed in a positive or negative direction, human needs and human tendencies drive the behavior.

When needs are being met, development follows a natural path. When needs are not being met, we see the three indicators of being off track—eddying out, taking a detour, and fighting the rapids.

Because Lily's fundamental needs were being met, Lily's charts show that her development was progressing positively.

Obstacles Point to Unmet Needs

In Sara's situation, some basic needs were not being met. Through observation, Sara's Montessori teacher could see that Sara was dealing with an obstacle to her development. Honest communication between Sara's parents and teachers about Sara's behavior helped identify the obstacle and Sara's unmet needs.

> *Unmet needs create obstacles to normal and happy development.*

Take a minute and look at the fundamental needs list. Perhaps you might see that these needs of Sara weren't being met due to Sara's parents' discord:
- Spiritual needs: belonging, acceptance, appreciation, celebration, closeness, community, emotional safety, empathy, honesty, love, reassurance, support, trust, understanding, warmth, communication, laughter, fun, create self worth, create meaning, order, harmony, and peace.
- Physical needs: protection from danger, sleep, and touch.

Humans get needy quickly. Our unmet basic needs create obstacles for our normal and happy development.

In our children's development, we need to be looking for unmet needs, not worrying if they made an A, B, C, D, or F in their classes.

What is measured is what is managed. We need to be looking for concentration and independence, the signs of natural and normal development, and the indicators of obstacles to development.

Emotions Are Need Driven

Feelings are another barometer of how our needs are being met. We need to ask our children about their feelings and physical sensations because emotions are need driven. Negative emotions serve as a wake-up call for us to understand that we have unmet needs.

Here is a list of some, but not all, negative feelings that signal unmet needs.

Negative feelings: afraid, agitated, angry, annoyed, apathetic, beat, bitter, blue, bored, confused, cross, dejected, depressed, detached, disappointed, discouraged, embarrassed, fidgety, furious, guilty, helpless, hostile, hurt, impatient, irate, jealous, lazy, numb, resentful, sleepy, uncomfortable, and worried.

Behavior and emotions indicate if needs are being met or not. When we can connect behaviors and feelings to unmet needs, we have a strong indicator of what we need to ask for to help make our lives and the lives of our children better.

When we can connect behaviors and feelings to unmet needs, the lessons we should teach become evident. The child's self-selected work becomes the healing agent by calming behavior, soothing emotions, and promoting healthy development.

> *When we can connect behaviors and feelings to unmet needs we know the lessons to teach.*

The Best Assessment Tool in the World

The assessment offered by a Montessori teacher in a Montessori prepared environment through observation of behavior creates the most important learning assessment tool available today. Grades can't approach the strength of astute observations that tell us how our children are doing and who our children are.

Observing the child at work in a prepared environment

The lessons that the Montessori teacher gives are another aspect of the guided observations of the Montessori teacher. Each lesson is presented at a specific juncture in the child's development. The *analysis of movement* during a child's activity gives important clues into the development needs of the child. Let's look at table washing, an activity in the Montessori primary classroom for three- to six-year-olds.

Table washing consists of a series of activities:

- First the child makes the decision to do table washing. The child's Montessori teacher has given the lesson previously.
- The child goes to the shelf and puts on the table-washing apron and finds a table to wash.
- The child returns to the shelf, gets the work mat, and places the table on the work mat.
- The child makes several trips to the shelf to get the wash basin, sponge, soap, brush, drying cloth, and bucket, setting each item in a precise spot on the work mat under the table.
- The child returns to the shelf to retrieve a pitcher in which to put water.
- The child pours water into the basin and proceeds to wash the table.
- When the child is finished, he or she returns each item to the shelf in reverse order, leaving everything ready for the next person.

Point of Interest

As we observe the child at work, we might see that the child struggles with several of the steps. Perhaps he spills the water or forgets to put a tool away. The teacher makes a note that she will need to present the work again, this time with a small twist, or *point of interest*, to emphasize the skill that needs strengthening.

A point of arrival for the child is the day when the child chooses and completes table washing (or any other task) and returns the materials to the shelf in good order while exhibiting the four following attributes of normalization:

- Love of work or activity
- Concentration
- Self-discipline
- Sociability seen in joyful work, mutual aid, and cooperation

The work is the test, and when we see these four attributes in the child, we know that life is going 100 percent okay.

Analysis of Movement

"Mike spills his milk at every meal—every meal for five years," Beth explained as she placed a kitchen towel on the table. I was visiting Beth, a childhood friend, who has seven boys. Mike is the youngest.

"How could a six-year-old knock over a glass at every meal?" I thought. Since I sat next to Mike, I kept my eyes wide open. After Mike took his first sip, I noticed that he placed his drink about an inch from the edge of the table, an easy and inevitable target for an elbow.

"Mike, I think if you put your glass right here after you drink, you'll be less apt to spill your drink." I picked up the glass, moved it above Mike's plate, and placed a coaster under his glass.

Mike placed his glass at the top of his place and had his first spill-free meal of his life. Mike's success stemmed from my use of two Montessori teaching techniques: analysis of movement and point of interest.

"Nobody ever showed me where to put my glass," Mike told me later. In the hub-bub of family life, nobody had ever analyzed Mike's movements.

Analysis of movement focuses on learning systems

Dr. Mel Levine in his book, *A Mind at a Time*, talks about eight basic neurodevelopmental systems. Each of us uses the following learning constructs:

- Attention
- Temporal-Sequential Ordering
- Spatial Ordering
- Memory
- Language
- Neuromotor Functions
- Social Cognition
- Higher Order Cognition

As we consider the table washing activity, let's analyze a child's movements and consider the neurodevelopmental or learning system to which the movement pertains. I hope that doing so will help explain these neurodevelopmental systems.

Neurodevelopment systems and movement

- If the child can't return the lesson to the shelf in the proper sequence, what does that tell us? For a three-year-old? A four-year-old? A five-year-old? A six-year-old? *Temporal-Sequential Ordering*
- What if the child forgets a step? *Memory*
- Does the child spill the water? *Neuromotor functions*
- Does the child get upset if someone bumps the table accidentally? *Social Cognition*
- Remembers every step and returns the materials to the shelf in good order? *Memory, Spatial Ordering, Temporal-Sequential Ordering*
- Places the materials on the wrong shelf? *Spatial Ordering, Memory*
- Does the child work with concentration? *Higher Order Cognition*
- Does the child work with independence? *Social Cognition, Higher Order Cognition*
- Does the child know the language to explain his or her work? *Language*

- Are the child's movements smooth and fluid, or does movement seem choppy and disjointed? *Neuromotor functions*
- How is hand and eye coordination? *Neuromotor functions*
- How is gross motor coordination? *Neuromotor functions*
- Does the child converse with others while carrying out his or her task? *Language, Social Cognition*
- Is the child aware of others while he or she works? *Social Cognition, Higher Order Cognition*
- Can the child verbalize a problem he or she might have while completing the task, such as running out of soap, and so forth? *Language, High Order Cognition*
- Does the child show problem-solving techniques, such as getting a mop to clean up a large spill? *Higher Order Cognition, Neuromotor Functions*

I use Levine's neurodevelopmental constructs here as a way of organizing the child's differing areas of development and how observing a very common activity in the classroom (or at home) can lead to deep insights into areas that a child might need help in strengthening.

Analysis of movement leads to deeper insights

The analysis of movement of the child at work gives us an insight where the child may be experiencing developmental difficulties and which learning systems may need strengthening through the use of the teaching technique of indirect preparation. The Montessori teacher can offer lessons in activities that would indirectly strengthen observed weak areas.

For example, if a Montessori teacher sees memory issues, the teacher might offer exercises with the materials called memory games as one type of strengthening activity. To aid with fine motor skills, the teacher might show brass or silver polishing to a child. For the child needing more social awareness of body movements, additional lessons in grace and courtesy are given.

To think in a straightforward manner about the Montessori teacher's work with the child in the prepared environment, we might look at it this way:

Observation
+ Prepared Environment
+ Pedagogical Principles
+ Knowledge of Developmental Continuum
= Optimal Learning and Growth in the Child

The power of a Montessori classroom begins with observation.

A Red Flag for Development

Each Montessori lesson has an age by which a child should be doing certain work. Chapter 3 contains a sample lesson from a teacher's album. If a child is not doing certain work by the indicated age, it is a clue that the child may be encountering a developmental obstacle. For example, if a child cannot wash a table by age four, this indicates a need for deeper observation of the child along with analysis of movement.

As parents, we want to be, as Dr. Mel Levine calls it, our children's "mindwatchers" and be on the lookout for any difficulties our children encounter. I promise, though I wish it were otherwise, there will be difficulties.

Parents' observations, Montessori teachers' observations, and our children's work over a three-year cycle create a detailed picture of who our children truly are—their likes, their dislikes, their strengths, their weaknesses, their opportunities, and their risks.

Grades can't tell us that. Only our observations can.

The Prepared Montessori Teacher

Montessori teachers are trained to observe and use personalized teaching *albums* which contain lesson plans for the age group in which they are trained. For example, the primary teachers have lesson plans for three to six-year-olds. In my experience, the curriculum contained in the albums for teaching three to six-year-olds contains enough lessons to keep a child busy with activities through at least a third grade level.

125

Elementary teachers' albums contain material to engage the mind up to a college level, if need be. My upper elementary class visited with the head of the geology department at our local university. The professor told their going-out chaperone that the elementary students asked better informed questions than his graduate students. This, I believe, was due to the research techniques the students had learned and used in their elementary classroom.

The botany work available in a Montessori elementary classroom covers more material than my sophomore level botany course in college. Montessori teachers have the lessons and the prepared environment to keep minds and hands engaged, no matter the age or talents of the child. For the child who needs additional time to learn or for the child who needs further challenge, the teacher's most important tool in working with the child remains observation.

As the prepared teacher in a prepared environment, I have watched children use their independence and concentration to do things some people might think impossible; for example, I have seen a child interested in math or reading jump four grade levels in two months. This kind of academic growth occurs because the child takes the independence and concentration developed in other activities and focuses on chosen tasks within a three-hour work period.

Teaching Based on Needs

Teaching to your child's individual needs and interests is the key to your child's success in school and in life. The paradox of Montessori teaching is that when we focus on a child's needs, we help the child develop into the kind of person who possesses the following qualities:

Happy	Giving	Confident
Self-motivated	Honest	Life long learner
Independent	Loving	Responsible
Empathetic	Respectful	Compassionate
Enthusiastic	World citizen	Resourceful

When a person possesses these personality traits, strong academic achievement is a by-product. High academic achievement is no guarantee of developing these human qualities. It is the age-old question: Which came first, the chicken or the egg? Academic achievement or strong character development?

Montessorians understand that helping children meet their fundamental spiritual and physical needs creates healthy human beings. Teaching to needs comes first. Achievement follows.

Nobody does it better than Montessori teachers.

What matters is not physics, or botany, or the works of the hand, but the will and the components of the human spirit which construct themselves through work. The child is the spiritual builder of mankind, and obstacles to his free development are the stones in the wall by which the soul of man has become imprisoned.

Maria Montessori

The Absorbent Mind, page 201

Measuring Academic Growth

Communicating academic skill levels to parents is one of the difficulties Montessori schools have. There are a few measuring sticks we can use to help us make sure that our children are meeting culturally determined norms in the basic skills of reading, writing, and arithmetic.

Keep your local public school standards handy

Because public educational standards vary from country to country, state to state, school district to school district, and year to year, it would be impossible for a Montessori teacher's training to take into account this multitude of standards to compare to each child's individual progress.

With the advent of the Internet, public school curriculum for most school districts is available online, though sometimes trying to find it is like looking for a needle in a haystack. Check with your state's department of education as well as your local school district to obtain a copy of your area's curriculum standards. Twenty years ago, I paid twenty dollars and waited six weeks for a copy of our state's public school standards. Today, most standards are available as a free download from the Internet.

Many Montessori training programs recommend that the public school standards be readily available to parents and the children in the classroom so that it is a simple process to glance over the standards for each grade level. I've visited many Montessori schools where the public school curriculum for the six years of elementary is kept in a handy binder in each elementary classroom.

In my classroom, each student kept a copy of the public school standards in his or her portfolio. When I saw a need, I'd review public school standards individually with my elementary students.

After a session reviewing public school standards, I was amazed and amused when my second-year seven-year-old students realized they couldn't do all the mathematical operations with fractions. Off they went to remedy the situation, gathering materials and asking for fraction lessons right away.

My experience is that when confronted with evidence that there is something essential they should know, children in a Montessori classroom will take corrective action. Parents as well as teachers need to communicate to our children our culture's standards as well as family expectations.

I admire this phrase used by Dr. Phil McGraw in his book *Family First*: "In our family we..." then fill in the quality, such as tell the truth, are kind to other people, work hard, want to learn, are curious, and so forth. Our children need for us to keep expectations clear and in the air. High expectations are the key to everything.

Portfolio assessment

Montessori elementary students keep an individual daily *work journal* that outlines the activities they do each day. Students are encouraged to keep samples of their work. In my classroom, the children kept notebook-sized portfolios. For large or group projects, we would take photos and add them to the portfolios.

Digital and video photography make the cost and ease of capturing images of the children's work much more manageable than ever before. Many schools maintain electronic portfolios where large posters, science projects, and videos of plays can be conveniently stored and accessed.

Portfolios can be peer- and teacher-reviewed and assessed in terms of criteria that are rubric-based. The peer and teacher assessment of work is more appropriate for the older child in the upper elementary classroom of the nine- to twelve-year-olds and the adolescent classrooms. We need to remember here that what gets measured get managed. Rubrics require thoughtful design.

Here is a student/teacher designed rubric developed to evaluate a report giving feedback on four areas: choice of topic, illustrations, spelling, and punctuation. The group then decides what level of work was accomplished: attempted, limited, proficient, or distinguished. Rubrics can communicate expectations for a quality project and give accurate feedback to students.

Assessment Criteria

	Distinguished 4 points	Proficient 3 points	Limited 2 points	Attempted 1 point
Choice of Topic	Choice of topic well thought out, and information gathered from many sources.	Topic meets assignment parameters, information is accurate.	Topic meets assignment parameters, information sometimes inaccurate.	Topic does not meet requirements. Many inaccuracies.
Illustrations	Well illustrated with meaningful and accurate drawings.	Illustrations aid in understanding.	Illustrations require more clarity.	Not enough illustrations or illustrations detract from presentation.
Spelling	Flawless.	Few errors.	Some errors in spelling and punctuation.	Many errors in spelling and punctuation.
Presentation	Visually enticing; good attention to detail.	Clear, attractive, uncluttered.	Legible.	Illegible or messy.

Standardized testing

Most achievement tests, such as the Stanford Achievement Test and the Iowa Test of Basic Skills, are curriculum-based tests, meaning that these tests were designed to test achievement around a specific curriculum.

Considering that the children in a Montessori classroom do not follow the curriculum that these tests use, it seems an oddity to test Montessori students using these tests.

Over the years I have administered achievement tests to Montessori students and others, using a variety of testing instruments. Interestingly I found that the student's grade levels shown on one standardized test correspond within a few months of another test. The difference in scores is not significant. For example, math computation skills might be 5.3 grade level on one test and 5.5 on another test taken during the same week by the same student.

Using a standardized test as an observational tool

Even if standardized tests are not administered to the children, the tests can be used as an observational tool by the Montessori teacher. The Brigance® Comprehensive Inventory of Basic Skills-Revised (CIBS-R) can be one such observational tool.

Understanding the skills assessment levels in the Brigance® (CIBS-R) along with observations and portfolio assessments, it is possible to determine a grade level for a child's basic skills in reading, writing, spelling, and arithmetic—*without having the student take the test.*

After administering and grading the Brigance tests a few times, I was conversant enough with the skills assessment that in an hour or less I could go through a child's portfolio and determine a grade level based on the work. For example, I could look at math problems and know that they were fourth grade level work. I could look at a child's writing and through misspelled words and sentence complexity give an accurate grade level for reading and spelling.

No surprises

I think that it is important for Montessori teachers to have a firm understanding of what type of work belongs to a grade level so that teacher, parents, and child are not surprised later on.

Twelve-year-old Jennifer's parents came back to complain to Jennifer's Montessori teacher after Jennifer's first grading period in junior high school.

"She's flunking English because she can't spell," said Jennifer's dad.

"But I've always told you that Jennifer wasn't a good speller."

"Well, we all thought she spelled well enough to pass seventh grade English."

Oops. Jennifer's parents and Jennifer needed a lot more tangible evidence than their Montessori teacher had provided. Jennifer's Montessori teacher, in terms of helping Jennifer understand her spelling weaknesses, hadn't been a help to life.

What can we, as parents and teachers, do to make sure there are no unpleasant surprises?

True confession time

With thirty students and being the school administrator among other responsibilities, I found it wasn't practical to individually grade level each student's portfolio, so I administered selected Brigance® (CIBS-R) tests in March over the course of a week for a half hour to an hour first thing each morning. I didn't see that this compromised the children's concentration and independence in any way. Some Montessorians might react in shock that I used these tests. So be it.

I would hope that this book will help parent and teachers develop skills to feel confident about student progress in order to *not use* standardize testing in our Montessori classrooms.

I used the Brigance® Tests for many years in my elementary class and saw that the children found the tests helpful as the tests gave them accurate and timely feedback about their skills. (The tests are teacher-scored.) The Brigance® (CIBS-R) showed my students the next challenge they needed on their academic path away from the Montessori materials and on to abstraction.

The results seemed to be the tangible evidence to help children's parents bridge the gap from their traditional schooling experiences to the different methods their children were experiencing in a Montessori school.

Standardized tests do not reflect the depth and scope of work that children in a Montessori school cover. For the amount of time needed to administer the tests and the cost of the tests, I've always thought that our financial resources could be better used. Our trips to our local arts center to see five live performances each year costs less than $25.00 per student. Most standardized tests cost upwards of $50.00 each, not to mention the costs of the time taken to give the tests.

The tests offered some pleasant discoveries. The Brigance® tests to an eighth grade level, and most of my ten and eleven-year-old students (fifth graders) reached the limits of the test.

As I mentioned before, how do you give grades for work that far exceeds your expectations as a teacher?

Many Montessorians do not use standardized testing in their classrooms, and I would prefer not to use them either, but I believe, if needed, that the tests can be done in an unobtrusive manner that acts as a help to life. My preference would be that teachers and parents understood academic milestones and cultural expectations well enough that observation of the child's work would be enough information to feel confident about academic progress.

If your child's Montessori school does not offer achievement tests, and you would feel more comfortable with tests, I recommend that you use a learning specialist to do so privately. The cost, usually under two hundred dollars for a privately administered test, will be minimal for your peace of mind.

For teachers, I suggest becoming familiar with selected Brigance® (CIBS-R) tests so you'll understand and be able to communicate your students' grade levels in core subjects without having to administer achievement tests. Curriculum Associates sell the Brigance® tests. Visit CurriculumAssociates.com.

Cultural literacy

Knowledge is partially culturally based which is another reason academic development can be difficult to communicate.

One of the important educational yardsticks I've used is E. D. Hirsch Jr.'s series of seven books targeted at kindergarten through sixth grade, beginning with *What Your Kindergartner Needs to Know.* The books are also known as the *Core Knowledge Series.* A recent addition to this series now includes the title, *What Your Preschooler Needs to Know.*

This series of books is well illustrated and serves as a yearly guide to each level of cultural literacy for children. Each book looks at specific knowledge in language, math, science, music, art, history, and technology for each grade level.

Copies of these books were in my elementary classroom for a quick reference. My students enjoyed perusing the books for ideas of topics for research projects or to test their own overall knowledge.

I encouraged parents to buy a book each year or to visit my classroom and browse through these books. The books give a general idea of the scope of ideas children should be exposed to for the next year, not just at school, but in all aspects of life.

Another of Hirsch's books, *Cultural Literacy: What Every American Needs to Know,* is a valuable resource. The appendix, "What Literate Americans Know", should be required reading for parents and adults in the United States. Hirsch's list creates a big picture of concepts for high school level cultural literacy. When I looked at it the first time, I discovered a few stumpers myself.

The Core Knowledge Series of books can help us view our children's progress in a way that helps child and parent know what the next step in literacy should be.

For more information about Core Knowledge, visit coreknowledge.org.

Ongoing parent education is essential

To help understand academic achievement in a Montessori

classroom, we've looked at public school standards, portfolio assessments, standardized testing results, and cultural literacy requirements. Let's look now at how Montessori schools can communicate an overview of a child's Montessori lessons to parents.

The only practical way is with ongoing *parent education* meetings where development is explained and parents are invited to do various lessons. A favorite lesson at parent workshops, based on the noise level at the tables, was finding the square root of numbers with the Square Root Board. Finding the square root of numbers is math that most of us did as eighth or ninth grade level work. Montessori first and second year elementary students can be quite nimble with using the square root board, with some students finding the square roots of numbers up to ten million.

> *Parent education meetings strengthen understanding of your children's work in a Montessori community.*

What? You never saw that problem on a standardized test? I wonder what percentile deducing square roots would put us in?

Request and attend ongoing parent education meetings to help strengthen your understanding of your child's work in a Montessori classroom. I think you'll be impressed with the sequence and scope of activities for your child.

Ask the important questions

As parents, we can get caught up in the trivial and pressing events in our family life and forget to do the important stuff. Take a quiet hour or so, perhaps once every month or two, and ask these questions about your child's development.

> *Is my child...*
> • Happy?
> • Confident?
> • Honest?
> • Independent?
> • Responsible?

- Respectful?
- Loving?
- Enthusiastic?
- Giving?
- Self-motivated?
- Enjoying learning?
- Financially responsible?
- Empathetic to others?
- Compassionate and understanding?
- Acting with integrity where values and action reflect each other?
- Seeing him or herself as a vital part of his or her community and the larger world?

Many Montessori parents are able to answer "yes" to most, if not all, of these questions.

Even if you answer "no" to one or more of these questions, understand that your child has encountered an obstacle to normal development. Obstacles are common, and their effects are inevitable. Obstacles, though, give us big clues into the needs of the child.

Remember, obstacles and negative emotions point to unmet needs. Once we understand obstacles and the nature of needs, we do what we can to remove these obstacles in order to aid a child's development.

No grades. No homework. No worries.

We should feel confident about our children not receiving grades or homework in a Montessori classroom when we
- understand the cultural standards in regards to our children's academic achievement,
- see that our children's work is the test,
- observe for the signs of natural and normal development, and
- watch for obstacles to development.

Being aware of public school curriculum, standardized testing, cultural literacy, and participating in ongoing parent education can keep us informed of our children's academic progress, which is a portion of our children's total development in terms of their mental, physical, emotional, and social/spiritual being.

We serve the future by protecting the present. The more fully the needs of one period are met, the greater will be the success in the next.

Maria Montessori
The Absorbent Mind, page 177

Homework

One of the central concepts of Montessori philosophy is the child's free choice to choose his or her own meaningful activities. Assigned homework doesn't allow for free choice. Therefore, most Montessori schools do not assign homework. What many Montessori teachers see, though, is children taking home their free-choice work and telling parents that they have homework!

We'll end the chapter with some thoughts about homework from my "Kids Talk" columns.

Rethinking Homework

Parents, imagine no homework to supervise and therefore no forgotten assignments. Teachers, consider having no homework to assign, grade, record, and monitor.

Alfie Kohn in his recent book, *The Homework Myth*, advocates abolishing homework based on a survey of educational research that shows there is no connection between homework and academic success.

For the past twenty years, under pressure to raise academic achievement, many school districts and schools have been increasing the amount of homework in hopes of raising standardized test scores.

Some homework advocates say that homework is about more than better grades or test scores. Time management, priority and goal setting, work ethic, study skills, and learning reinforcement are also given as reasons for assigning homework. Kohn reviews research that shows, again, that there is no correlation between homework and these skills.

Kohn asserts that educationally we have been duped.

Having been an elementary teacher who didn't assign homework, I found it curious what my students would choose to do at home. Afraid that their children would sit in front of the television, parents at first were skeptical of my no-homework approach. Over the years, my students' parents reported that their children chose to read, do math problems, write in their diaries, create plays, have pen pals, and more when given a choice about how to spend their time and energy. Parents reported that their children cheerfully helped prepare dinner and clean up afterwards. That was a refreshing and positive outcome for not assigning homework.

What our children, our families, and our teachers need is a choice of how to effectively spend their time in order to meet the needs of each person, family, classroom, and school.

Imagine if after the school and workday our families only had to worry about how to best spend their newfound time. Imagine no conflict between parents and kids over when to do their homework, where to do it, how to do it, and why it isn't done. Imagine having time at home to devote to helping our children and family develop practical life skills of cooking, home care and maintenance, conversation, problem solving, and critical thinking.

Teachers, imagine if you had no homework to assign, collect, grade, and record. Wouldn't it be wonderful to choose a more effective way to communicate progress in your classroom? Perhaps to write a one-page letter once a month detailing the highlights of your classes' work? Or perhaps have a two-hour parent/student open house twice a year for students to show off their classroom, friends, teachers, and school? Could no homework free teachers up to give each student's parents a ten-minute phone call a couple of times a year? Would no homework give teachers more time to plan lessons? Learn new skills? Spend time with their families?

There are many things we could do to better serve the needs of our children, our families, our teachers, and our schools than assigning homework.

It's time to rethink the effectiveness of homework and the important dynamic relationship of home/school/child. We—parents, teachers, and school administrators—need to stop and examine the homework myth.

True Homework: Building a Home Life

Many people are astounded when I tell them I didn't give homework to my elementary students. There are many reasons I didn't give homework, but the main one is fairly simple. The reason for coming to school is to work and learn. If students are doing what they are supposed to do in school, which is to work and to learn, and if my job is to create an environment where children "yearn to learn," does assigning homework help me meet my objectives in the classroom? Does homework help the children become better learners?

The time that children spend at home should be spent in activities that strengthen family relationships. As adults, most of us would resent being sent home with an hour or two of work, day after day, after we had put in a full day on the job. Why do we think our children will feel differently?

I share parents' concerns of children not using their time wisely if there is no homework to keep the children busy. Here are some suggestions that can help direct a child's activity during home hours while nurturing that "yearn to learn" and building family bonds.

- Encourage your child to write weekly to grandparents, aunts, uncles, cousins, and out-of-town friends.
- Keep a five-hundred-piece jigsaw puzzle as an ongoing project. I used to keep ten loaners in my classroom closet.
- Do crosswords puzzles. Friends of mine do the crossword puzzle in the New York Times each week as a family. It usually takes all week, but every time someone walks past the puzzle on the kitchen counter they try to add a word.
- Play board games as a family. Some recommendations are checkers, chess, Outburst Junior, Pictionary Junior, Scrabble, Jeopardy, and Rays of Light. Ask friends for recommendations.

- Develop a family hobby. My brother-in-law's family collects antique toys. A friend works with her daughter on dollhouse miniatures. Find something that interests you, and encourage your child to help. You will be developing a lifelong bond. That's important homework.
- Encourage your children to help with meal preparation and clean up. Fix dinner as a family instead of "taking turns" or leaving one person to do all the work.
- Designate one evening a week as "Family Night" and do something as a family. Taking a walk, skating, biking, playing tennis, making craft items, or watching videos are fun family night activities.
- Monitor television viewing and watch as a family. Plan what television shows or videos will be watched during the week. I kept a small lending video library at school with books that complemented the subject such as National Geographic Specials (*The Titanic*), *Sarah, Plain and Tall*, or *The Secret Garden*, for example. Watching a video can stir a child's interest in a subject, and a handy book will help the child explore his or her curiosity.
- Read books out loud. A chapter a night is fun, and everyone can take turns reading a chapter. Jim Trelease's *The Read-Aloud Handbook* is a good resource.

The work of the child at home is to build a home life. These activities can help bring families together while still satisfying and strengthening the child's "yearn to learn."

CHAPTER SUMMARY

In terms of our children's growth, we need to measure human qualities that are important to life. Academic achievement is only a small part of our children's development and may actually be the skills we should measure last.

In Montessori classrooms the child's work is the test of whether certain skills and interests are developing. The Montessori teacher's task is to observe the work of the child and guide the child's development with the next challenging activity.

With normal human development, we see people who have a love of work or activity, an ability to concentrate, self-discipline, and a sociability seen in joyful work, mutual aid, and cooperation.

Obstacles to development are numerous and are characterized by three types of behaviors:
- Eddying out
- Detouring
- Fighting the rapids

Observations of behavior and emotion are key to helping a child on a healthy path of development. Behavior and emotions are need driven and give important signals to the unmet needs of the child.

Montessorians see that helping children meet their fundamental spiritual and physical needs creates healthy human beings. Teaching to needs comes first. Achievement follows.

In Montessori classrooms we can measure academic growth by understanding societal norms and relate them to the work of the child. The homework of the child should be to build a home life.

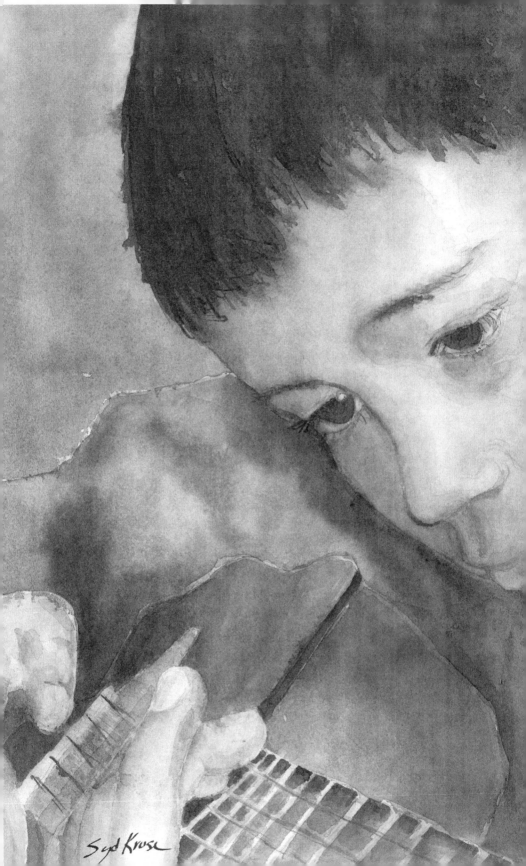

Syd Kruse

Chapter 6

Finding a Quality Montessori School

Finding a School that Fits Your Family's Needs

Before you think about a specific school, there are important issues that should be considered. Understanding these sometimes subtle matters will help make your school choice more thoughtful, more comfortable, and in the long run, more successful.

The first item we need to consider in finding a quality Montessori program is the needs of your child, along with the needs of your family. This chapter is to help bring to your awareness these needs. Our family needs questionnaire will help you begin focusing on finding a good school match for your family.

Montessori schools come in all shapes and sizes, from a classroom in a teacher's home to a multi-building complex with several hundred students. As you explore different Montessori environments, you'll find differences and similarities. The differences will be based on meeting the needs of the children in that school at that time with the resources available. The similarities should be schools trying to implement Montessori philosophy in the best way they know.

The Education Equation

That brings us to what I call the "education equation." For a child, or a person for that matter, to reach their highest potential, many factors need to be considered into this basic education equation:

$$\text{Child} + \text{Parents} + \text{Teachers} \Rightarrow \text{Adult}$$

A child working with parents and teachers becomes an adult.

Perhaps we could also state this equation as:

$$\text{Child} + \text{Home} + \text{School} \Rightarrow \text{Adult}$$

A child working within an environment that includes home and school becomes an adult.

More simply said is this:

$$\text{Child} + \text{Environment} \Rightarrow \text{Adult}$$

A child working within his or her environment becomes an adult.

Why an Education Equation?

Why, you may ask, bring up all this business about an education equation?

My hope is that the education equation will start you thinking about the multitude of variables that exist in your child's education and how you might control those variables.

First, we'll look at a child's developmental needs, then we'll consider what factors home and school play in our education equation.

> $\text{Child} + \text{Home} + \text{School} \Rightarrow \text{Adult}$
> *A child working within an environment that includes home and school becomes an adult.*

Factors in the Child's Development

As we consider the needs of the child, we need to look at factors inherent in your child's character and factors that are external to your child.

Internal factors

When considering inner characteristics of your child, ask these questions:

1. **Is your child outgoing or more reserved?**
2. **What plane of development is your child?**
3. **Is your child having a physical response to the environment?**

Elements to consider here are allergies, illness, learning or perceptual differences, hearing, vision, diet, sleep, changes in routine, visitors in the house, family member out of town, death in the family, birth of a sibling, arguments in the family, television viewing, or video/computer games.

> *A child working within his or her environment becomes an adult.*

External factors

When looking at a child's external factors in our education equation, we need to ask the following:

1. **Does your child's environment offer an opportunity to work in peace and dignity?**
2. **Does the environment offer a wide social experience?**
3. **Does the environment offer protection from physical and psychological harm?**
4. **Does the environment offer adequate challenges for personal growth?**

Your child's development is affected by how these factors are minimized or maximized in his or her education equation.

Factors in the Home Environment

As parents, we are our children's first and most important teachers. To be most helpful to our children, we need to become "enlightened adults," or people who are observant and understand child development concerns.

The internal and external factors affecting our children also affect us as parents. As adults, we should be in the position to be able to control and modulate many of these needs in our own lives and the lives of our children.

What factors maximize our role as parents in our child's development?

1.   Are we prepared to be parents?
Have we considered our own character to uncover any shortcomings that might cause us problems in dealing with our children?

2.   Do we use our imagination to visualize the "person who is yet to be" in our child?
Here I refer to the kind of character and values you wish for your child to have, not what profession or career you want your child to have.

3.   Do we look for clues in our children's activities to help us know how to help them?

4.   Do we bring an attitude of respect for the personality of our child and his or her task of building a person?

5.   Do we try to see the world from our child's point of view?
Chapter 9 will focus on us, as parents, seeing from a child's perspective.

Factors in the School Environment

The teacher component
In the education equation, parents must include the child's factors with their own. The teacher's considerations include the child and parents' factors, along with a Montessori teacher's commitment to be a "help to life."

As parents, I think we want teachers who have asked themselves the following questions:
1.   Am I prepared to be a teacher?

A teacher needs to look at his or her character and make sure there are no personality obstacles in dealing with children.

2.   Have I prepared an environment in which the child can reveal his or her true nature in order to show me how to be of help?

3.   Do I help and guide the child in constructive activities?

Teachers should encourage and direct activity, never forcing or discouraging purposeful behavior.

4.   Do I see myself as the most vital part of the child's school environment?

At first it is the adult's appearance that gains the child's confidence and respect. A teacher needs to be as gentle and graceful as possible. Under fire, the teacher must be calm and dignified.

5.   Do I observe the child engaged in activity, watching for independence and concentration?

The school component

The school component of our education equation must encompass and balance the needs of the children, parents, and teachers it serves. The school component is evident through the school administration, policies, and underlying philosophy.

1.   Does the school respect the needs of all the children?

2.   Does the school have clearly stated goals and objectives, including curriculum?

3.   Does the school have clearly stated expectations for behavior and outcomes for children, parents, teachers, and others involved in the school community?

4.   Does the school create a clear structure for the community to interact positively?

5.   Does the school provide an overall atmosphere of nurturing families?

The school environment plays a major factor in a child's development, and we need to control what elements we can to be advantageous to our children's growth.

147

> Child + Home + School ⇒ Adult
> *A child working within an environment that includes*
> *home and school becomes an adult.*

Including Time and Money in Our Education Equation

Now that we've finished an overview of our education equation, we need to include two large factors that affect almost everything in life: time and money.

$$Time \times Money \times (Child + Home + School) \Rightarrow Adult$$

As you look for a learning environment for your child, even if you aren't aware of it, you will use the education equation to make your choice. If you were aware of how to use the equation to find the best learning situation for your child, well, wouldn't that be awesome?

Let's take a look at how the factors of time and money might affect your decision-making process in choosing a Montessori program that is right for you.

Money

Montessori programs can vary in cost from around four thousand dollars per school year for a half-day program for three- to six-year-olds in the Midwest to ten thousand dollars for half-day primary programs in large cities. Annual tuition for residential farm school programs for twelve- to eighteen-year-olds begin at the twenty-five thousand dollar range and go up to fifty thousand dollars.

As you consider Montessori programs, I suggest you put the money issue on the back burner until you have considered the needs of your child and your family, visited at least three facilities, and observed several classrooms. Don't limit your prospects by saying before looking, "We can't afford it," or "We can only budget this amount." Go through the selection process with a mind open to all possibilities. Looking at a range of prices will help you see the true costs of a program and perhaps be understanding of programs that cost half to a third as much as other programs.

To use our restaurant analogy, knowing what you have to pay at five-star restaurants can make a home-cooked meal seem more appetizing. However, selecting the most expensive place may meet your needs more closely. As a friend of mine says about costs, "You can get where you want to go in a Volkswagen or a Mercedes. It's about how you want to travel." Invest the time to find out about different programs. It'll make you a wiser consumer.

Many of the more expensive schools have scholarship programs or reduced payment plans for which you might qualify. There may be public Montessori schools in your area. For some families, homeschooling using Montessori methods is an option that is the best alternative. I've known several families who have opted to send a parent through Montessori teacher's training as an investment in their children's education.

Time

Time may actually be more important to consider than money. Consider the time it takes to get back and forth to school. There is also the amount of time that your child and family will spend involved with the school.

Some parents drive many hours getting children to and from school. If this time commitment requires hours in a car per day, you'll need to assess how viable that is for the long term. Perhaps moving closer to the school is a long-term strategy or carpooling with school families in your neighborhood. Too much time fighting traffic can sour even a wonderful situation. Be careful of how much time you commit to commuting.

How many years of Montessori education do you want to plan for your children? Only preschool? Through kindergarten? To third grade? Through middle school? High school?

We live in a transient society, and the idea of knowing where we'll be living in five years is impossible for many of us. Even if you think you may move cities or change schools, take the time to consider the overall benefits in each stage of your child's and family's Montessori experience.

In my early days as a Montessori parent, I watched as a transfer student, a four-year-old boy, entered the classroom for the first time. The boy walked around the classroom one time, chose a piece of material off the shelf, walked to a table, and went to work. Like a fish to water, or perhaps I should say like a koi to water since the boy was Japanese and didn't speak a word of English. Even in a new culture, he seemed right at home in a new Montessori classroom.

As you think about schools for your children, from preschool to high school, remember to use the education equation:

Time × Money × (Child + Home + School) ⇒ Adult

Family Needs Questionnaire

Let's put these ideas to work for us now by using a questionnaire about your family's needs. This questionnaire will help you consider your child's needs, as well as the needs of parents, siblings and other family members.

You can download this Family Needs Questionnaire at MarenSchmidt.com.

Thoughts on the Family Needs Questionnaire

Once you've answered the family needs questionnaire, let's look at some of the implications in terms of your family's needs.

1.   What stage of development is our child? Birth to three, three to six, six to twelve, twelve to eighteen?

As mentioned in Chapter 2, your child is on a continuum of development divided into four stages that last about six years each. Understanding the natural characteristics of the child during each of these stages of development will help you select the best learning environment for your child.

2.   Is our child naturally outgoing or more reserved?

In his book, *The Optimistic Child*, Martin Seligman, Ph.D., explains how a child who is not naturally outgoing or who tends toward pessimism can be helped to be more social and optimistic by the guidance provided by parents and teachers. Making sure you have a satisfactory match of teachers and school philosophy will help bring out your child's best qualities.

3.   Does our child have allergies to medications, foods, or other substances?

If your child has allergies, such as to dust or peanut butter, it may be difficult to find a school that has an allergy-free environment. How a school handles allergy issues will be a concern to you.

4.   Has our child's hearing and vision been tested for difficulties?

Hearing and vision issues are the most common causes for developmental delays. Before your child starts school, it is a good idea to make sure that your child's sight and hearing are not impaired in any way.

5.   Is our child a picky eater? Which foods does he or she avoid?

As your child enters a school environment, his or her favorite foods may not be served at snack or lunch. Also, if your child avoids certain foods, this could indicate allergies to those foods or that your child may have some sensory issues with food for texture, taste, or temperature that may need to be addressed.

6.   Does our child eat a well-rounded diet?

Children who do not eat a breakfast with both high-protein and complex carbohydrates show lower levels of concentration than children who do have a nutritional breakfast. Sugary cereals, fruit juices, donuts, and other high sugar foods can short-circuit the learning process.

7.   Does our child get ten to twelve hours of sleep per day?

Many children and adults do not get enough sleep. Children between the ages of three and six years usually require ten to twelve hours a day. Some children may require closer to fourteen hours per day. Running on a sleep deficit can make your child cranky and unable to make the choices necessary for optimum learning.

8.   Have there been any changes in routine in the past

month or two? For example, a move to a new house, birth of a sibling, parent traveling, long-term visitors in the home, death in the family, job loss, job change, parent separation or divorce, arguments in the family.

If your family has had a lot of changes in the past few months, your child may not be ready to make yet another change by starting school at this time. Depending on the temperament of your child and other family factors, your child may be best served by waiting a few weeks or months to start school. As you visit with schools, be sure to mention the issues that may be affecting your family.

9. **How many hours per week does our child watch television or movies?**

If your child watches more than two hours per day of television or movies, he or she may find it difficult to actively engage in a classroom situation. Before entering school, get television and video viewing down to two hours per day, preferably less.

10. **How many hours per week does our child play video or computer games?**

Again, if your child plays video or computer games more than two hours per day, he or she may find it difficult to actively engage in a classroom situation.

Children should be limited to two hours or less of all electronic media per day. My experience has been the less electronic media a child under the age of six uses, the happier and more focused the child's behavior.

11. **Does our child have a long-term illness? Has our child had a long-term illness in the past? For example, chronic ear infections or asthma.**

As you select a school, be sure to let the school know about the sorts of health issues your child has or has had in the past.

12. **How many hours per week does our child ride in a car?**

Some parents are so accustomed to an hour commute to work that they don't think about how sitting may be affecting their child. If your child has a long ride to school, let your school know. Many schools that have children with long commutes will try to make sure there are opportunities for large movement first thing in the morning if they have this information.

13. How many people per week does our child interact with?

The child who is an only child in a quiet home environment with limited interaction with other children may find starting school overwhelming. Given perhaps an adult's undivided attention and no experience dealing with children who may or may not do what he or she wants, an only child can find school an overpowering experience at first.

14. Do we feel that our child has adequate challenges for personal growth?

As mentioned above, an only child may find the beginning social challenges of school intense. The three-year-old with teenaged brothers may hear and repeat language that is not included in typical preschool vocabularies. The child who has natural talents or special needs may require an environment that stimulates development in vital areas.

15. Is our child in an environment that protects him or her from physical and emotional/psychological harm?

As you visit schools, you will be in a position to see how the adults treat the children, how the children treat the adults, how the children treat other children, and how adults treat each other. Do children and adults treat each other with kindness and respect? Are there clear guidelines and expectations for behavior and how to handle conflict?

16. Does our child have daily opportunities to work, learn, and play peacefully in a child-based environment?

Too many times our children's developmental needs are subjugated to the needs of the adults in the child's environment. The child's place to work, learn, and play can become adult-based fairly quickly if we aren't careful. Music, games, activities, and conversations that are not peaceful or developmentally appropriate may be presented to the children based on the needs of the adult instead of the needs of the child.

A vivid example for me of crossing this line happened when I visited a childcare center at lunchtime. The staff had a big screen television tuned to a soap opera during lunch with two-and three-year-olds. Was this a child-based or adult-based environment?

Parents' and family needs

1.   Are we emotionally ready to let our three-year-old go to school?

2.   Are we in a position to support our child emotionally in a new situation?

3.   Have there been any significant changes in our lives in the past two months, such as relocation or a new job, that could affect the emotional center of our child?

As discussed above in Question 8, there can be various situations that may make it challenging for your child to start school at a specific time. Having your child start preschool during a time of upheaval may not be the best thing for your child or family.

4.   Is our family physically ready for school? Is our child on a sleeping and eating schedule that works with the school schedule?

If your family runs on a different schedule, be aware that you may want to transition into the school timeframe. I had a three-year-old student who had a very difficult time beginning school because he had never gotten up before 8:00 a.m. and school started at 8:15. He was cranky and didn't want to get out of his car in the mornings.

5.   Is our child recovering from an illness or on medication that could make him or her drowsy, cranky, or hyperactive? Some allergy medications and antibiotics affect alertness and energy levels.

Be sure to read about the side effects of any medication your child may be taking. The side effects, such as sleepiness or irritability, could alter how your child reacts to a new situation.

d _

6. **Are all members of the family—siblings, parents, and extended family—positive and excited about this first step into a larger world for our child?**

"If momma ain't happy, ain't nobody happy," goes a homespun adage. We could add Aunt Hilda in there. Be sure that your child feels everyone's excitement about his or her going to school. Tensions have a way of popping up in the strangest places and at the most inconvenient times.

7. **Do we need before and/or after school care for our child?**

As you search for a school, be clear about what hours your family needs.

8. **Do we have a backup plan for our jobs when our child is ill or school is closed due to inclement weather or school breaks?**

Take a few minutes to think through how you will handle picking your child up from school when you get called as you go into an important meeting or if you are out of town when the school closes for an ice storm.

When my daughters were in preschool, I acted as backup for a friend who was a homecare nurse and whose husband was a surgeon. Think who could be your backup if needed.

9. **How many hours per week do we need to drive our child to school? Does this impact our family life adversely?**

At one point in my children's schooling, I drove five hundred miles a week to get them back and forth to school. After a year, the two hours a day in the car started to get old. Think through the long-term implications of your decisions.

10. **Is our family budget strained by paying for private school?**

There are young families who feel the peer or family pressure to have their children attend a preschool that they cannot afford. If school tuition will be more than half your house payment, you may need to rethink how much you are paying for tuition or a house payment.

Explore options for financial assistance at the schools you visit.

Also, be sure to consider charter and magnet school options in your area.

If your child's grandparents are in a position to help pay for tuition and have offered to help, don't be too proud to take them up on the offer. Over the years I have known grandparents who were truly thrilled that they could help get their grandchildren off to a good start in life.

A friend's in-laws chided her about the amount of money she was spending on Montessori preschool. "You should be using that money for a college fund," they said every time they talked on the phone. When they visited after a few months of school, they apologized after hearing their three-year-old grandson sing a song naming the continents and count to ten in French after serving them cookies with the phrase, "Would you care for a cookie, Granddad?"

"Please," they said, "let us pay for his Montessori school as long as you want him there. We can't think of a better way to invest our money."

And so they did.

11. Do both parents feel that school tuition is a wise investment for our family?

Both parents need to be committed to their child's education with both time and money. Remember the education equation? If one parent is not committed, there will be tension in the relationship, and more likely than not the child will be pulled from a program as that parent becomes more and more dissatisfied.

Be fair to your child, the school, and your marriage. Make sure you have commitment from all parties concerned.

12. Is there enough time and money in the family budget for us as parents to pursue some of our interests?

It's no fun to have every penny in your budget earmarked for your children and not any for you. Keep yourself interesting by making sure you give yourself enough time and money to pursue your dreams.

13. What indicators do we need to feel confident that our child is making satisfactory progress in his or her development?

Many Montessori schools do not give grades. I've seen parents grow dissatisfied with their elementary Montessori programs because of this lack of grades and feeling uncertain about their child's progress. For myself, I've felt a twinge of competition as I've seen my neighbor's children's names on the honor roll when my children's reports were a vague "making progress."

In Chapters 3, 5, and 8, I hope to give you enough information about how to judge on your own that your child attending Montessori elementary is making strong progress in his or her overall development, including academics.

Other family members' needs

14. How will our child attending preschool affect other family members? Siblings? Grandparents? Others?

Think about how the changes will affect your child's siblings and others. Grandparents can become a little teary eyed as they have less time with their grandchildren after they start school.

15. Are other family members supportive of our child going to preschool?

As discussed above in Questions 6 through 12, be sure that all family members are supportive of your child going to school.

16. Will the time needed to transport our child to school adversely affect other family members?

Teenagers, who get upset and angry because they have to be dropped off early or picked up late because of their baby brother or sister going to preschool, can be resistance that you hadn't anticipated.

I appreciate the motto "Forewarned is forearmed."

Hopefully, working through this needs questionnaire has forearmed you so that you will be prepared to find a school situation that matches not just your child's, but your entire family's needs.

Next is a "Kids Talk" about getting ready for preschool. Then we'll look at matching your family's needs with a school.

Getting Ready for Preschool

Mornings are cooler. The sun rises later. The excitement of school beginning wafts in the air. These are my memories when school started in mid-September. In two or three weeks, school resumes, and for many young children, it will be their first school experience.

The first day of preschool or kindergarten is probably more traumatic for Mom and Dad than it is for our Emilys and Erics. Preschool is our first big step in letting our children go, if only for a few hours a day. As parents, we wonder, "Will they do all right without me in a new situation?" The question we need to ask is, "Will I be okay when I leave them?"

Most children take to preschool like a duck to water. The children who have difficulty adjusting usually have parents who are having trouble making the change.

Betsy's mom dropped her off with the parting words, "If your tummy hurts, Mommy will come and get you." It doesn't take too much imagination to figure out which preschooler had a stomachache every day for two weeks. Her mom said, "I guess she's not ready for preschool."

Brewster threw a tantrum every day upon his eight o'clock arrival to school. After a few days, I learned that this three-year-old had always slept until eight thirty each morning.

Tomas resisted getting in the car to come to school. After a phone discussion with his father, we discovered that his grandmother, who had lived with Tomas all his life, had moved away two weeks previously.

To make the adjustment into preschool easy on your family, ask these questions:

1. Are we emotionally ready to let go?

Do we have a plan of what to do with our time when our child is in school?

2. Is our child emotionally ready for a new situation?

Have there been any significant changes in our lives in the past two months, such as relocation or a new job that could affect the emotional center of our child?

3. Is our family physically ready for school?

Is our child on a sleeping and eating schedule that works with the school schedule? Also, be careful to not return from a week or two vacation a couple of days before starting preschool.

4. Is our child recovering from an illness or on medication that could make him or her drowsy, cranky, or hyperactive? Some allergy medications and antibiotics affect alertness and energy levels.

All members of the family should be positive and excited about this first step into a larger world. A few days before school starts, arrange to take your child for a fifteen-minute visit to his or her school in order to meet teachers and become familiar with the facilities.

On the first day, exude the message, "I know you'll have fun," by saying a quick good-bye and leaving with a smile, even if you feel like crying through every pore in your body. You'll also need this advice in twelve to fifteen years when leaving children at college.

In my twenty-five years of experience, children cry when separating for less than two minutes. For a mom and dad, it's a long two minutes, but two minutes just the same. If children cry for over five minutes, it is usually because they are running a fever, didn't get enough sleep the night before, are hungry, or all of the above, which helps make a clear-cut decision about whether to give a child more time to calm down or to send a child home.

After you leave your child at preschool, have a plan for that morning—join friends for coffee, grocery shop, go to work, and so forth. My project was to take a shower by myself for the first time in four years.

Enjoy being the parents of a preschooler. It's exhilarating, exhausting, and exceptional. Enjoy. Your preschooler will be e-mailing home from college before you know it.

Matching Your Needs with a School

We've spent some time looking at the needs of your family. There are all kinds of things to juggle when deciding on a school: how you feel about a school, what you think about a school, how much time it takes to get there, how much money, how large the commitment, if the school offers the before and after care you might need, if it offers elementary and junior high opportunities, and most importantly, if it is a good match for your child's personality as well as your family's values.

As we've mentioned before, schools come in different shapes and sizes. One Montessori friend teaches at a school in California that is mainly a Hindu community. The entire school meditates for the first hour of the day. Yes, they are an authentic Montessori school. Another friend teaches nine- to twelve-year-olds in a large eastern city. Family expectations are that the children will go to elite college preparatory schools, and the upper elementary curriculum includes getting ready for entrance exams. This school, too, is a quality Montessori program. Another friend runs a twelve-student program in her walkout basement. Each one of these is an authentic Montessori program that uniquely meets the needs of the children and families it serves.

It doesn't take too much imagination to see that the California students might not be happy in the East Coast school and that the East Coast folks would not select the school with meditation or the small school in a basement. For the children who attend these schools, though, it is obvious by watching for a little while that the children are engaged in purposeful activity and that they are joyful workers.

Essential Elements

Each of these programs, though they look very different from each other, shares the same basic standards. These essential elements, as we've discussed before, of authentic Montessori classrooms and schools are:

1. Adults professionally trained in Montessori philosophy,

methods and materials for the group they are teaching

2. Prepared environments based on three-year age groups
3. Children's free choice of activity within a three-hour work cycle.

Focusing on these three elements will be your biggest help in finding a quality Montessori school.

We're ready to find schools in your area to visit.

How to Locate Schools in Your Area

Personal recommendations

Probably the strongest recommendations for schools will come from your friends, family, and coworkers. Take these recommendations seriously. These people know you, care about you, and more than likely share many of your same values and concerns.

At our first orientation meeting for our new primary class, every parent knew at least two other people in the room. The surprising thing is that no one knew the others had enrolled. They all had mutual friends who had children in Montessori programs in other cities and had recommended they come and look at our school.

Keep your ears open for recommendations from friends, family and coworkers.

Web-based searches

In today's world, the fastest and easiest ways of locating schools in your area is to do a Web search using "Montessori schools" plus the name of your town or zip code. Also, use the links to national Montessori associations given on the next page.

Yellow pages

The yellow pages of your phone book are also a good place to locate schools. Look under private schools, preschools, and daycare centers. And, of course, look under "Montessori schools."

State childcare licensing agencies

Check with your local department of human services office or

Web site in their childcare center area. There may be small programs that do not advertise in the yellow pages or appear on other Web sites, such as my friend who has twelve students in her walkout basement. If you live in a small city or rural area, this might be the best way to locate a program.

National Montessori Associations

These sites list schools in your area, based on the school's credentials:

Association Montessori Internationale (AMI/USA)
Amiusa.org
(Look under the AMI Schools heading.)

American Montessori Society (AMS)
Amshq.org/schools.htm

The Montessori Foundation
Montessori.org/schools/search.php

North American Montessori Teachers Association (NAMTA)
Montessori-namta.org

Public School Montessorian
Jola-montessori.com/search/

There are 275 public Montessori schools and 120 charter Montessori schools in the United States as of December 2008. The *Public School Montessorian* and the Montessori Foundation sites will help you locate not only public, but all Montessori schools in your area, regardless of their affiliations.

Visit three schools

Visit a minimum of three schools. If there is only one Montessori program in your area, visit other non-Montessori programs so that you will be confident that you are getting the program that best meets your needs. Visit your public kindergartens and schools or other preschools so that you can have some comparison.

Unfortunately, not every Montessori program is a quality one, and you may find what you need in another situation. It pays to be well informed.

Use our checklists

Chapter 7, Visiting a Montessori School contains checklists and other decision-making criteria to make sure you focus on the essential elements of an authentic Montessori school, large or small, along with the aspects necessary for identifying any quality program, Montessori or otherwise. I wouldn't want you to miss the best burger place in town because you thought it wasn't a serious food place. I wouldn't want you to miss a great Montessori school because it may not be the most expensive or largest one in your area.

With the information presented in Chapter 7, you'll have the tools to find a serious Montessori program, large or small, expensive or affordable, public or private.

CHAPTER SUMMARY

There are many factors in how a child develops. We might look at these factors as an education equation with several variables. These variables include the child and the child's environment of home and school.

Time and money are two factors that we need to consider to balance our education equation.

As you choose a school for your child be sure to look at specific needs in regards to your child, your family members and yourself. Use our needs questionnaires to become more aware of these needs and think how you might be able to meet and balance these different needs.

Chapter 7

Visiting a Montessori School

Setting Up the Visits

Using the information in the previous chapter locate at least three schools that you would like to visit. If there is only one Montessori school in your area, visit other schools, either private or public, and use these same checklists. It is important to know that you have made your decision based on as much information as possible.

Call each school and ask about their enrollment and visiting procedures. Most schools now have Web sites that give you information about the school's visiting and enrollment policies.

Some schools may not do initial one-on-one visits and may instead offer open houses at different intervals during the year.

One-on-one visits

Call each school and arrange for a visit. Ask each school how much time you should allow for a tour. Morning visits are recommended if you want to see a preschool classroom in action. Three- and four-year-olds usually are in a morning half-day program. This means you will probably have to do the visits over at least two or three days to allow yourself adequate time.

Open house visits

Inquire about the format of the open house visit so that you can be prepared to gather information. Some open houses start with a group meeting and a tour of each classroom, allowing for time to visit with staff and administrators.

Surprise visits

Some childcare advocates recommend surprise visits to schools. That is fine if you want to get an insight of how the school runs when company isn't expected. If you expect a tour and someone to spend an hour or more with you, make an appointment. School administrators are busy people, plus there is always the risk that, without an appointment, the children won't be in school that day for some reason.

Checklist: Things to Ask

Remember, you are asking questions for a long-term situation, not just for your child's immediate needs. You may want to bring these checklists with you, of course, or you may feel more comfortable filling them out afterwards in your car or at home. You might also be able to answer many of these questions from the school's Web site and brochures.

Some of these questions may appear invasive. It is better to have a long-term view of the school you select for your children. It is not ideal for your children to be pulled out of a program after a few weeks or months because you weren't aware of certain policies or procedures. It is to your advantage and the school's best interest to invest the time in the beginning to have a good match.

The School Visit Questionnaire is available on-line and may be downloaded from my website: MarenSchmidt.com.

Let's Look at What You Discovered

You've gathered a lot of information. You might have been so well prepared about looking at schools that you've already signed up.

If you are still in the decision-making process, read on. If you've made a decision, you may want to look at the factors that helped you make your decision.

For those of you who like to have a numbering system, for each question give a 1-2-3 score to each question:

> 3 — for exceeds expectations,
>
> 2 — for meets expectations, and
>
> 1 — for does not meet expectations.

With the 60 questions on our list, a score of 180 would mean that the school exceeded your expectations on every item. Scores between 180 and 120 show that that school exceeded or met your expectation on most things. A score below 120 indicates you have areas of concern. A score of 60 or below shows that the school was a dismal failure in your opinion.

You'll probably be pleased with a school with scores between 180 and 120.

Please note that this scoring is subjective in the sense that value is given based on whether *you* think the school met *your* expectations. Another person may get a very different score for the same school, so I wouldn't necessarily compare scores but instead compare findings. The questionnaires might lead to some interesting discussions of differences, such as, "Why did you think the school building was not in good repair?" and so forth.

School Visit Questionnaire Scoring	
180	Indicates that every aspect of the school exceeded your expectations
180–120	Indicates that all aspects met your expectations
120–60	Indicates that many aspects of the school *did not meet* your expectations

Let's take a look at what some optimal responses may be. Note that the longer a school has been established, the higher likelihood of certain policies being established and well thought out. Smaller programs and schools may not have as developed a structure or policy as older and larger schools, but they may offer a more personal setting for your family.

After reviewing your school visit questionnaires, look over your family needs questionnaire. With this information you should have a clear direction for selecting a school.

School Visit Questionnaire Revisited

General questions

1. What's the daily routine?

Your school tour guide should be able to tell you how the children enter the building, how they enter their classrooms, and the routine for dismissal. A good sign is if your tour guide also mentions a three-hour work cycle in the routine and how snack and lunch are handled. In a strong Montessori program, you are looking for free-choice activity in a three-hour work cycle.

2. How many children are in a classroom?

Traditional thinking is that the fewer students per teacher the better. Not so in a Montessori program. In a well-running classroom, a maximum number of children promote a richer learning experience. Twenty-four to thirty-six children in a classroom provide a vibrant setting for children.

Most Montessori programs are also required to meet state-mandated childcare guidelines. These guidelines dictate the child-to-adult ratio in a classroom. The size of the room also dictates the number of students in a classroom. The number of students in a classroom may be smaller than the recommended number due to these state guidelines. Another reason for a smaller group is accommodating school growth. Your tour guide should tell you about this.

3. What is the age mix? What is the mix between boys and girls?

A strong Montessori program should begin the school year with a mix of about a third of their students being age three, a third age four, and a third age five. There may be six-year-olds in the primary program due to state mandated cutoff ages or due to the school's sensitivity to the four planes of development.

4. How do you ensure that the children have a three-hour work cycle?

A strong Montessori program will run a three- to three-and-a-half-hour morning session. It is not unusual for the school to have a policy that children need to arrive by a certain time in order that each student can reap the benefits of a three-hour work cycle.

5.   What types of training do teachers have? How many years of experience does each teacher have?

The teacher in your child's classroom should have an appropriate training for that level with AMI or MACTE credentials. For example, a primary classroom should have a trained primary teacher, and an elementary classroom should have a trained elementary teacher.

If this is not the situation at the school, look a little closer. If a primary teacher is teaching elementary, is the teacher involved in a summer elementary training program?

Having a first-year teacher is not a reason to feel apprehensive. Inquire about how new teachers are mentored at the school. If all the teachers in the school have less than three years of experience, you may want to inquire more about staff development.

6.   What is your policy about sick children?

If the school is part of your childcare plan, this is a very important question.

Overall absences due to illness are significantly less in organizations that send sick people home quickly. A well-defined sick policy helps keep all the families in the school healthier.

7.   How are birthday and holiday celebrations handled?

If you have religious concerns about holidays and birthdays, now is the time to find out about how they are handled at this school. Most Montessori schools are sensitive to diversity and celebrate it.

Some schools may downplay holidays and focus on maintaining a three-hour work cycle for the children. Others may have day-long celebrations.

8. **What is the school's discipline policy?**

The school should have a clear discipline policy and expectations for behavior for staff, children, and parents written in a parents' school handbook.

9. **How does staff handle a biting incident? Hitting incident? Name-calling incident?**

Your tour guide should be familiar with how these incidents are handled. These kind of incidents should not be ignored or excused, and the school should have some form of adult intervention and coaching for problem solving with the children.

10. **Do you have an anti-bullying policy and training? Are all staff members trained?**

Since many Montessori schools have a peace curriculum, the words anti-bullying may come across as harsh to the tour guide. Your tour guide should be able to explain how the school creates and ensures a safe environment for all children.

11. **What is the school's attendance policy?**

Woody Allen's comment that 80 percent of success is just showing up applies here. Many schools have policies that if your child has more than two weeks of unexcused absences, your place in the school may not be secure.

A strong Montessori program is going to require attendance in order for your child and all children to obtain maximum benefit from the program.

If your family spends large amounts of time away, now is the time to inquire about attendance requirements.

12. **May I have a copy of the parent handbook?**

The parent handbook should outline the important policies of the school and help solidify your tour. The school should have extra copies or offer to mail you one. Many parent handbooks are available at a school's Web page.

13. **How accessible are teachers and other staff members?**

Many schools now have teachers accessible to parents via e-mail after school hours. Parents have different needs about communicating with their child's teachers. Some schools, in order to avoid abuse of their teachers' classroom or time, have restrictive policies.

If you ask to have a conference with your child's teacher or a school administrator, they should get back to you within forty-eight hours to set up a convenient meeting time.

14. How are parents informed of a child's progress? Learning difficulties?

Your tour guide should be able to tell you about how and when progress reports are given to parents. Strong programs usually assess a new student's progress during the first ninety days and let parents know if there are any concerns.

15. What steps are taken if a child starts to lag behind his or her peers?

Montessori teachers are trained to observe the child at work and are trained in the developmental steps a child makes working in a Montessori classroom. A child-paced Montessori curriculum allows for the teacher to emphasize and give lessons with various points of interests to the child who has not reached certain milestones.

A strong program will offer parent education meetings to help parents become aware of these milestones. Parent education meetings also offer suggestions to parents on how to aid the child's development.

16. What if my child needs to have more challenging work?

The beauty of a Montessori classroom is that it is prepared for all kinds of challenging work. A trained Montessori teacher, observing the child at work, should pick up cues and offer adequate challenges. The classroom for three- to six-year-olds easily accommodates at least a third grade level of work.

17. How are parents involved in the school?

Schools vary in the amount of day-to-day parent involvement they encourage. A strong school offers opportunities for parents to become involved at whatever level they are comfortable—for example, reading aloud to children, making materials, fundraising, driving on outings, and going to parent education meetings.

18. How does the application process work?

The application process can vary greatly from school to school. Some schools have a rolling enrollment. Others only accept new students in September and January. Some may have parenting classes to attend as part of the application process. Be sure to ask so that you aren't surprised.

Elementary Questions

1. When do you know a child is ready to move into your elementary program?

Strong Montessori programs allow children to transition to elementary as they show developmental signs of being ready to leave the self-mastery emphasis of the primary to the group-work orientation of elementary.

State mandated childcare regulations may require that children move to elementary based on age cutoff dates, for example, that a child must be six years old by September 1 of that school year.

In some situations, children are developmentally ready to go to elementary and can't because their birthday falls after the cutoff dates.

Another issue about going to elementary is that parents "push" to have their child go to elementary before the child is developmentally ready.

2. Is your elementary a Montessori program or more traditionally based?

Some excellent Montessori primary programs feed into non-Montessori-based elementary programs in their schools. There can be many reasons for this. The main reason is that the lack of trained elementary teachers keeps schools from having a Montessori elementary program.

There are some Montessori schools that offer authentic Montessori programs only for their primary programs. For various reasons, some of them quite valid, their elementary and middle school programs are not Montessori based. This can come as a bit of a shock to some parents of six-year-olds, who may be expecting a Montessori elementary program.

3.   Are elementary teachers trained at the elementary level?

Again, finding trained teachers can be difficult for schools that are located a distance from a training center. It's best to clarify the school's situation as early as possible so that your expectation of their programs is realistic.

4.   Is homework assigned in elementary?

Traditionally Montessori programs do not assign homework. The paradox is that students will take work home and tell parents they have homework.

Some upper elementary classrooms for nine- to twelve-year-olds do assign homework as a help to the children who will leave to go to traditional junior high or middle school.

5.   How are the basic skills of reading, writing, and arithmetic emphasized?

Your tour guide should be able to tell you about how the elementary curriculum develops these skills or be able to provide you with information describing the elementary curriculum, either Montessori-based or traditionally based.

6.   How do the lessons in elementary provide a rich content?

The lessons in elementary are designed to capture a child's imagination. The elementary curriculum integrates all subjects. For example, the "Story of the Creation of the Universe," also called "God with No Hands," is a first week of school lesson that incorporates the laws of physics and chemistry with hands-on demonstrations that the children can do as free choice activities. From that story, the children may connect with work in math, language, the arts, and of course, the sciences.

Again your tour guide should be able to provide you with examples of the richness of the curriculum or provide you with a brochure.

7.   How much physical activity do the children get per day?

When the school facilities allow for it, children should be allowed free movement between the classroom and out-of-doors.

Programs may incorporate physical education in their free-choice activities using yoga or calisthenics command cards.

8. Do you have an outdoor classroom? How is outdoor time handled?

Many Montessori classrooms strive to make the indoors and outdoors flow into one continuous workspace. In many Montessori schools, the outdoor component of the school's vision is substantial. The tour guide should be able to tell you how that works if the school has an outdoor classroom.

9. Are there any after school activities?

Montessori programs come in all shapes and sizes. Some offer before and after school care and activities. Others have school-only hours. Others allow organizations such as Girl and Boy Scouts to meet after school or allow private music, art, or dance instruction in the building after school hours.

10. Do elementary students take standardized tests, such as the Iowa Basic Skills, Stanford, and so forth?

Many Montessori schools use standardized tests to help parents and students feel confident they are meeting societal expectations. Some Montessori purists feel that standardized testing is not warranted. Others are realists, knowing that parents need a level of comfort that their student is working at or above grade level. Your first visit is a good time to ask how a school approaches this issue.

11. How do the elementary students perform on the standardized tests? Do you have written documentation that you can share with me?

Montessori elementary students, in general, perform well on standardized tests, especially when you consider they are not "taught to the test." If the school's vision includes using standardized tests, a strong program should be able to provide you with how their students performed overall.

12. How does the school encourage creativity? At the preschool level and elementary?

A strong Montessori program feeds the elementary child's

imagination while developing creative skills of art, music, movement, and drama. Your tour guide should have anecdotes of plays, building projects, illustrated stories, and more.

13. Does the school have a program for twelve- to fifteen-year-olds? If not, where do the children go?

At this writing, the twelve- to fifteen-year-old Montessori programs are growing by about fifty new programs per year with approximately three hundred fifty "adolescent" programs now running in the United States.

Montessori students make a predictable academic and social adjustment to junior high or middle school. If they did well (meaning, did they show all signs of *normalization*) in Montessori school, they do well in junior high. If they didn't show signs of normalization in their Montessori work, they'll more than likely struggle with junior high. Transitions therefore should not be a surprise to parents or students.

14. Does the school have plans to establish a middle school/junior high program?

If you are a new entering family with a three-year-old, it might be nice to know if the school is planning a program or not. This question helps you know what to expect down the road and if the school fits your family's long-term needs.

School Questions

1. What do you think are the school's strengths? What do you consider to be the school's weak points?

This question will help you ascertain if the school's administration has given some thought to these issues. In many ways it doesn't matter what they say are strengths or weaknesses. It's important that they have spent some time thinking and articulating what those strengths and weaknesses are.

What the school might see as a strength, you might consider a weakness. The evidence of a thinking process is key.

2. What Montessori professional standards does the school follow: AMI (Association Montessori Internationale), AMS (American Montessori Society), MACTE (Montessori

Accreditation Council for Teacher Education), IMC (International Montessori Council) or other? Does the school administrator have commitment to Montessori practices?

A school's professional Montessori standards should be evident. There are schools that follow certain standards but may not be accredited by the training institutions. Schools that are located near training facilities are more likely to have accreditation by the major Montessori organizations. For example, AMI accreditation requires that all teachers in a school have AMI training. For schools located many miles away from training facilities, that requirement is a big hurdle.

If a school is near a training center and is not accredited, it is probably a more important question than for one that is two hundred or three hundred miles away from a training center.

School administrators should be committed to Montessori practices even if they are not trained Montessori teachers.

3. How is the school administration structured?

Is the school privately owned or a 501 (c)-3 not-for-profit entity? How long has the school been in business? If the school is privately owned, you might want to inquire about the owner's retirement plans. Schools may close when the owner retires.

4. If the school is board governed, how are board members selected?

How the school is governed is a key to its stability in regards to keeping effective administration, teaching staff, and happy families. A board that is too heavy with parents with currently enrolled children may be fixed on the short-term needs of their children and not have the best interests of the total community in clear view. On the other hand, if a board is comprised of individuals with no understanding of Montessori education, programs may suffer.

A board with fewer members and with longer terms is generally more effective than a larger board with shorter terms.

5. How is policy adopted?

Policy may be decided by the board or by the school director.

This is good to know before you have any problems.

6. How are grievances handled?

The school should have a formal written procedure for how grievances are to be addressed.

7. What kind of staff turnover rate does the school have? How long has the present director been involved with the school? The previous director?

A high turnover rate might indicate school management problems. On the other hand, there are well-managed programs with low turnover rates where everything happens at once. Stability of the staff generally indicates a well-run program.

8. How does the school ensure that they have trained teachers?

Strong programs usually sponsor one or two teacher trainees on an ongoing basis, especially schools not near a training center. Sponsoring teachers, by offering financial support over the training period in return for a minimum amount of service, helps create a stable and consistent Montessori program.

9. What training do classroom assistants have?

Classroom assistants should have at a minimum in-house training before entering the classroom.

10. Does tuition cover all expenses of the school?

Parents are often surprised and then irritated if the school is not well funded and constantly solicits funds. Many schools depend on a certain level of fundraising from their families. Again, this is a good thing to ask at the beginning.

11. Is there fundraising? How is that done?

Again, this is good information to have in the decision-making process.

12. Does the school offer financial assistance? If so, how does that work?

Most schools that offer financial assistance give information on their Web site or in their parent handbook about the process of applying for financial assistance. Some schools have a philosophy that financial assistance is designated for long-term families who are experiencing a need due to a job loss, illness, or other situations. Other schools try to have an economically diverse school population and offer scholarships to those families who show a commitment to Montessori education for their children.

13. What would you say is the overall philosophy of the school?

Strong programs should be able to tell you who they are. Look for a mission statement in the parent handbook.

14. How do you think a parent can best help the school community?

This is a question that helps you know how much thinking the school community has done on this issue.

Overall impressions

People

1. Did the staff answer your questions in a polite, friendly, and informative manner?

2. Did staff seem genuinely interested in your family? Did you meet the school director? Do you feel you can approach the director with concerns, if necessary?

3. Are all teachers Montessori trained? Is the school director Montessori trained?

4. Are there specialists for art, music, foreign languages, and so forth?

These four questions are designed to help you think about the level of commitment the people involved with the school have. A strong program has strong commitment from all levels in the community, families included.

A note about specialists: strong Montessori programs try to use specialists as little as possible and encourage classroom teachers to develop skills in areas such as art, music, and foreign language. It's difficult to maintain three-hour work cycles and accommodate specialists. It's not impossible, just difficult. So you may hear that the classroom teacher is the specialist.

Classroom

1.   Did you see inside a working classroom?

2.   Did the children appear to be actively involved in their work?

3.   Did the three- to six-year-old classroom seem calm and orderly?

4.   Did the elementary classroom seem noisier and more active while the children seemed engaged in small group (two to six children) activities?

These questions should help you think about if you enjoyed seeing the children working even though it might not be the way that you went to school. Are you comfortable with the learning process you saw in the classroom?

School

1.   Were the classrooms clean, attractive, and well-lit?

2.   Were the bathrooms clean?

3.   Were the outdoor areas attractive and safe with a variety of activities?

4.   Is the building in good repair?

5.   Are there assigned areas to observe classrooms?

6.   Was there anything that just didn't feel right to you?

7.   How would you describe the school's overall atmosphere?

These questions will help you reflect on your overall school impression. Sometimes we might be impressed with the people and the classrooms but have a feeling of dissonance because a facility wasn't as clean or attractive as expected. It is not an impression that should be lightly dismissed. The overall atmosphere reflects the values of that community. If you experience dissonance, the school may not be the right one for your family.

One more important item

Check with your state's childcare licensing division to make sure that the school has no serious complaints or problems pending. If you've used this questionnaire, you'll have a good idea if the school is likely to have any situations that would violate your state's childcare standards.

Do You Have an Idea of What You Want?

If you walk away from a school visit feeling positive, it's probably because all the factors we examined here mesh with your expectations of meeting your child's and family's needs.

Be sure that you've gathered the information about the application process. This varies greatly from school to school, and a school administrator should be happy to help you understand their procedures.

At this point, you should have a good picture of the school you would like for your child to attend.

In *Chapter 8, Assuring Success,* we'll look at how you can best utilize your child's, as well as your own, experiences in a Montessori school.

CHAPTER SUMMARY

Visit at least three schools, Montessori or otherwise, to give yourself an idea of what is available in your area.

Use the school visit questionnaire to gather information that will help you have some insight into the culture of the school.

Chapter 8

Assuring Success

Understanding Three Key Ideas Supports Success

To effectively support your child's Montessori education, there are three key issues that I think you might want to understand. I wish I had understood them better. I would have avoided a lot of headaches and heartaches if I knew then what I know now. As they say, hindsight is always 20/20. Perhaps you can benefit from my look in the rearview mirror on understanding these concepts:

- The idea of free choice in Montessori philosophy
- Having a big picture of your child's education
- Knowing that life is problems and how to solve many of them

Free Choice

Montessori philosophy can benefit every child. Unfortunately, Montessori philosophy doesn't work for every parent. For the over twenty-five years I have been involved with Montessori education, I've observed that parents who become dissatisfied with their Montessori experience don't understand, much less accept, a central tenet to Montessori philosophy.

What is this critical idea?

The exercise of free choice, specifically the child's free choice.

Two freedoms

Charles Kingsley, the English novelist, wrote that there are two freedoms, "the false, where a man is free to do what he likes; the true, where he is free to do what he ought." Montessori education seeks to develop "true freedom" where freedom is linked with responsibility.

Parents who don't understand the difference between "false freedom" and "true freedom" may become frustrated if they see their child's development of responsibility as stifling and "not doing your own thing." There are parents who think that Montessori philosophy means to "let it all hang out." These parents see the Montessori idea of "freedom within limits" as too restrictive for their tastes. These parents have a more permissive parenting style.

On the other side of the coin, parents who use external control to force their children and others to act "responsibly"—instead of helping the child develop inner discipline—can become dissatisfied with a Montessori classroom. As their children learn independence and responsibility, parents may feel like they lose control over their children.

There are parents who find it extremely difficult to allow their children the opportunity to earn independence and freedom. For this reason they have problems with Montessori education because they cannot find the balance between order and chaos. We might say these parents have an authoritarian parenting style.

When we, as parents, can link freedom with responsibility, we can feel confident that as a child's self-discipline increases, we can decrease our direct parental control. Montessori parenting is partnership parenting.

Being free to do what we ought to do within limits of responsibility is true freedom.

Freedom within limits

Dr. Montessori advocated freedom within limits, with limits enlarging as the child's experience and responsibilities grow. Dr. Montessori wrote, "On this question of liberty, we must not be frightened if we find ourselves coming up against certain contradictions at every step. You must not imagine that liberty is something without rule or law." (E. M. Standing, *Maria Montessori: Her Life and Work*, page 286).

One limit of freedom is that "the liberty of the child should have as its limit the collective interest; as its form what we usually consider good breeding." Dr. Montessori saw that good social skills were imperative for the child to be able to function freely in the prepared environment of the classroom, at home and the larger world. In a Montessori classroom, the child who disturbs other children while they are working will find that his or her activity is restricted.

A second limit is that knowledge must precede choice. There is a fundamental difference between curiosity and true choice. With curiosity the child is drawn to a novel object or activity in order to acquire more information and understanding. Once curiosity is satisfied, the child acts in order to grow instead of only to know. A child may be curious about a certain lesson in a Montessori classroom and the teacher's presentation of the materials may satisfy the child's curiosity. When the child chooses the lesson off the shelf after this initial presentation, the materials are worked with in order to discover more about the activity. This is the moment when true learning begins.

This difference between satisfying a fleeting curiosity and true choice is the reason behind the Montessori rule that a child needs a lesson from the Montessori teacher before using a material. This prerequisite helps the children "like what they do" instead of "doing what they like."

A third limit is that the materials must be used correctly, meaning that the child's work with the materials leads the child to order, harmony, self-development, and discipline. Activities that lead to the dissipation of the child's creative energies—which leads to disorder—need to be guarded against. A child who imagines pencils to be airplanes and throws them across the classroom will bump into this limit on his or her freedom.

A fourth limit is the number of materials in the environment. The prepared environment of the Montessori classroom creates a limit on the kind of activity the child can do. In a way, the children have chosen the materials in a Montessori classroom. Today's Montessori activities have endured the test of time by being interesting to the children, as well as helping the children develop concentration. The child who wants to bring a new toy or computer game into the classroom will likely run into this restriction.

Defining freedom

Ask ten people what freedom is and you will get at least ten different answers. There are at least that many definitions in the dictionary.

The first five usages given in *The American Heritage Dictionary* for freedom follow:

- The condition of being free from restraints;
- Liberty of the person from slavery, oppression, or incarceration;
- Political independence;
- Exemption from unpleasant or onerous conditions;
- The capacity to exercise choice; free will.

This idea of freedom is a little mind-boggling. Do we have it? How do we keep it? Do we want it? Can we give it? Can we accidentally take it way? What happens if we take it away on purpose? What definition should we use for freedom?

Let's examine a few ideas on freedom.

"Freedom is the oxygen of the soul."—Moshe Dyan

Dyan, the Israeli general, uses the fifth definition of freedom, "the capacity to exercise free choice," as being the fuel of our deepest being. This ability to choose feeds the flame of human existence. It is this type of freedom that Montessori urged us to protect and nurture in the child.

"We must be free not because we claim freedom, but because we practice it."—William Faulkner

Faulkner, too, uses the definition of free will when he writes of freedom. We can't sit around and say we are free or that we live in a free country. We must practice freedom. We must use our capacity to choose or lose this thing called freedom. Faulkner places a lot of responsibility on our exercising this ability to choose. Dr. Montessori saw the right to choose as essential to the development of healthy humans.

"Freedom is not worth having if it does not connote freedom to err." —Mahatma Gandhi

With freedom, Gandhi again refers to our capacity to choose. Borrowing terms from the other definitions of freedom, our fear of failure creates personal prisons, sentences us to a "form of slavery or oppression", and exiles us to "unpleasant or onerous conditions." These adult fears create a tyranny for a child. We are human; we make mistakes. Humans are the problem creators as well as the problem solvers. It is best that we remain friendly with error. Dyan's pure oxygen of the soul allows us to make mistakes and dissolves the bonds of fear, granting us the power to fail and to learn.

"There are two freedoms—the false, where a man is free to do what he likes; the true, where he is free to do what he ought." — Charles Kingsley

Kingsley's version of freedom uses the definition of free will and our ability to choose. Gandhi and Kingsley understood that in exercising our ability to choose, we will err. Being fooled by false freedom is easy because it beckons us with pleasantries. When we are allowed to "do what we like" instead of "liking what we do", true freedom linked to responsibility is lost.

Freedom comes from first recognizing order, harmony, self-development, and discipline, then developing those traits though practice. True freedom lies in having the strength of will to create a life based on universal principles of truth, justice, courage, humanity, compassion, forgiveness, and understanding.

The principles of a Montessori classroom support the child's developing capacity to exercise choice and develop free will. This freedom in the classroom forms a foundation of a positive psychology for the young child that bears fruit evidenced in the child's expression of individuality, self-discipline, concentration, and independence.

Freedom for the adult

In his book *Choice Theory*, Dr. William Glasser writes about his fifty years of work helping people understand their personal choices. Glasser maintains that all of our actions, feelings, thoughts, and physiological symptoms stem from our choices. We choose our response to everything in our lives. As soon as we become aware that we are unconsciously choosing unproductive or hurtful outcomes, we can begin to see the choices we have in every situation.

Glasser's book tells of people who have found the power of choice to set them free. The woman who becomes migraine-free. The asthmatic man on his deathbed who understands how his choices have made him ill, and so he chooses to live. The couple who sees how their choices can support or destroy their marriage. Glasser says, "A choice theory world is a tough, responsible world; you cannot use grammar to escape responsibility for what you are doing."

The grammar referred to is the difference in these two sentences:

"You make me so mad."

"I choose to be mad at you."

Using choice theory, we become the subject and not the direct object of our lives. With choice theory, we take responsibility for our actions, our thoughts, our emotions, and the physiological symptoms for those actions, thoughts, and feelings.

Glasser shows us how choice is an essential component of being a healthy and loving adult. Montessori principles light the way to help the child exercise choice, thus allowing the child to develop in a healthy, responsible, and loving manner.

If you choose Montessori education for your children, choose it for yourself as well. Learn and understand choice and choice theory and its role in creating true freedom in the child and the adult. That is one way to assure success with your child's Montessori education.

Seeing the Big Picture

If you understand the relationship between choice and freedom, the role freedom plays in a Montessori classroom, and how the child's free-choice work with the materials leads the child to order, harmony, self-development, and discipline, the next two items—the big picture and problem-solving skills—may appear insignificant.

The wave hits

It happened to me. I've watched it happen to others. The year that your oldest child turns three, an unsettling realization occurs: I'm playing for keeps! It's been three years, and we've just begun. Three years down and the rest of my life to go! This is a big commitment. What have I done?

This surprise wave knocked me over, filling me with claustrophobic panic. This third year of parenthood is a hard one on marriages as the long-term realities—financial, emotional, and physical—of being a parent become undeniable.

My moment of truth came twenty-five years ago when I realized I wanted to be, and I needed to be, a more conscious parent. That commitment to parenthood, I feel, has made me a better person.

A difficult lesson for me was about making a commitment to our children's education. Our first Montessori school was for one- to six-year-olds. The nearest Montessori elementary program was a thirty-minute drive from our home. When Dana was one, I wasn't thinking about kindergarten. I was more concerned with bedtime routine, toilet training, and Hannah on the way. Elementary school? Sorry, it wasn't in the top fifty on my list. We took school day by day, month by month, year by year.

Now that I'm on the other side of raising children and all the things in between, I wish that I had seriously considered the Big Picture. Considered? I didn't have a clue.

We buy cars and make three, four, five, or more years of payments. Homes come with thirty-year mortgages. Our children are going to have at the minimum thirteen years of schooling from kindergarten through high school. When you add in college and preschool, you may be looking at twenty years of schooling. We're talking a substantial amount of time and money. That money may be in terms of your tax dollars spent for public education, after-tax dollars for private education, or some combination of both.

Either way, the investment of time and money in our children's education is huge. I feel the whoosh of the Big Picture Wave hitting me right now. For thirteen years of public K–12 education costs range from around $120,000 per student in states like Massachusetts to around $80,000 in Mississippi. Our tax dollars pay for public schools, and those thousands of dollars are being paid by you, the tax payer. Private school costs vary from lows of around $3,000 per year to over $50,000 a year for residential junior high and high school programs, as well as college. The amount of money needed to educate a child can take your breath away.

I'd like to take a moment to say thank you for being a parent. It takes an enormous sense of courage, optimism, and humor. Thank you.

If you choose a Montessori education for your children, commit to a minimum of a three-year cycle. I've talked with parents who wanted to put their child in for only one year when the child was four. That was the money and time commitment they thought was reasonable.

Children benefit substantially from one year in Montessori school, though most schools have policies that try to discourage one-year enrollments. One-year enrollments do not take advantage of the long-term potential a Montessori school has to offer an individual child or the other children in the program. As I told one dad, "With a one-year enrollment, it's like you want your son to play varsity ball for only his junior year, get a scholarship, and then go and play ball in college. That strategy doesn't make for a good team, and it doesn't let your son develop his full potential as a ball player. Why do that to your four-year-old?"

In this case, using a four-year-old may be a poor example as many Montessori schools only admit three-year-olds or younger or admit four-year-olds only if they lose a student. Some schools are vertically integrated, meaning once your child is admitted, the school guarantees a place for him or her for the entire time. For a school with an elementary program, the school is making a nine-year commitment to each student.

When you see your child's schooling as a long-term commitment, your child, your family, and your school benefit in powerful ways, ways that schools and families with short-term commitments can only dream of.

Also, when you see your children's schooling with a long view, certain options may seem feasible, such as opting for a smaller home, a less expensive car, or investing college savings in your children's early years of Montessori school. With an eye to the long term other possibilities that may not be readily apparent come into focus, such as establishing a Montessori charter school, taking Montessori training, or homeschooling the Montessori way.

Helping families gather enough information to consider a long-term plan for their children's education is the main reason for this book. My experience shows me that dedicated and focused families create optimum schools and situations, which in turn nurture children in the best possible ways.

Having my family involved in Montessori education has made our lives richer. I would wish the same for you. If that is your choice. Remember, free choice.

Problem-Solving Skills Support Your Child's Montessori Education

Let's face it: life is problems

A new three-year old student was having a difficult time during the first week of school. At a conference I requested, Jacob's mother, Gena, looked at me through red-rimmed eyes. "I thought your Montessori school would be a place of calm and protection for Jacob."

"What do you mean, a place of calm and protection?'" I asked.

"I thought Jacob wouldn't have any problems here because it is such a calm and peaceful place."

"What problems do you think Jacob is having right now? What is happening at home?" I said.

"His dad and I are fighting, and Jacob's hearing things he probably shouldn't. His older brother has gone to live with his father, my first husband. Jacob's older sister left for college. My husband's father, Jacob's grandfather, who always lived with us, died a month ago. And now his grandmother is in the hospital."

I caught my breath as I realized the emotional turmoil in three-year-old Jacob's life during his first week of school. Life is problems, and Jacob's family was experiencing a lot of life at the moment. No wonder Jacob was hitting children and having temper tantrums.

"Stop the world," Jacob was trying to tell us. "I want to get off."

Gena thought that all of the upheavals in Jacob's life would end as soon as he walked onto our school campus, that somehow the tall walnut trees would shelter him.

Unfortunately, problems have a shadowing property. Wherever you go, there they are.

The best we can hope for in our lives is to have people who will help us work through our problems—not protect us from them or handle them for us, but assist us compassionately when we have to deal with tough stuff.

As I visited with Jacob's mother, I tried to help her see life from Jacob's point of view. In the course of a month, a beloved grandfather had died. Jacob's older siblings had left home, leaving an emotional hole as though they, too, had died. His grandmother was in the hospital, and Jacob couldn't visit. On top of all that, his parents were fighting and yelling things like, "I wish you were dead."

Jacob's mother burst into tears. "I never thought about it that way. I know his father doesn't see it this way either. We have to stop fighting and help Jacob."

We talked about what Jacob needed to feel emotionally secure again. We agreed that Jacob should take a week off from school, spending time at home with his parents, talking everyday on the phone with his siblings and grandmother, and seeing his parents make up and hug. Jacob could then start the school year fresh from a new emotional center.

Hopefully, you won't have problems as concentrated as Jacob's family. But you should realize you will have some type of problem. Financial setbacks. A job layoff. An illness in the family. A learning challenge with your children. Conflict and misunderstandings. How you handle these issues will affect you, your child, your family, and more.

Too many times, families under stress make decisions and react before they have time to work through a problem—decisions that in the long-term may not be in the best interest of the child or the family. Many times this short-circuited reaction is due to there not being a built-in problem-solving mechanism in an organization, be it a school, business, family, or couple.

If you have a problem that involves your child's school, I would hope you would use this five-step problem-solving technique. This technique can also be used in any type of situation.

Problem solving in a school setting

Direct, open communication is necessary for a healthy school community. When encountering a problem, address the problem directly with the person who is most affected, using the following five-step problem-solving technique.

If you feel it is inappropriate or awkward to approach the person directly involved, visit with the school director about the situation.

If your problem is not resolved after working through the problem with the school director, or based on your school structure, contact a member of your organization's board or write a letter to the board stating the problem with possible solutions and recommendations.

If the issue is not remedied to your satisfaction, you will have the self-assurance that you did what you could to solve the situation. At this point, you have two choices:

1) Graciously accept that your solution was not what the school director or board decided was best for the entire school community; or

2) If you cannot live with the problem and/or the solution after working through the process, you probably should leave the school in as kind a manner as you can muster. If the school's values and your values are not aligned, any other actions on your part will be seen as agitation, which does nobody any good.

Here is the five-step problem-solving technique that can be used at work, at home, at school, at church—anywhere and everywhere there are problems. The good news is that this problem-solving technique works. We only have to remember to use it!

Five- step problem-solving technique

Step One: I think we have a problem. Talk to the person directly involved with the problem. Ask the person if he or she is willing to work on the problem.

Step Two: What is the problem? Define the problem as clearly and specifically as you can. Commit to a win-win situation from all parties involved.

Step Three: What are all the solutions to the problem? Brainstorm through all the possible ways to solve the situation. Make a list even if some of the solutions seem unfeasible.

Step Four: What is the best solution? The problem solvers select the best solution and agree on how to implement it.

Step Five: Check back: Is it working? The problem solvers check back with each other and use observation and questioning to make sure that the solution agreed upon is meeting the needs of those involved.

If not, then go back to step one and go through the process

again.

An example: Suzie doesn't want to go to school

Suzie, a four-year-old, doesn't want to go to school. She cries in the morning when getting ready and says that her teacher doesn't like her. This is Suzie's second year in this classroom, and Suzie has always enjoyed going to school. Suzie can't tell her parents about any specific incident that occurred.

Step One: I think we have a problem. Suzie's mother, Joan, visits with Suzie's teacher and tells her that Suzie has been upset the past week and doesn't want to go to school. Joan tells the teacher that the only reason Suzie can give for not wanting to go to school is that her teacher doesn't like her, even though she cannot give a specific incident. Joan asks the teacher, Martha, if she is willing to work on the problem of trying to figure out what is bothering Suzie.

Step Two: What is the problem? Joan and Martha work to define the problem as clearly as they can, writing it down to help see it clearly. They define the problem in this way: Understand why Suzie doesn't want to come to school and what we as teacher and parent can do to help Suzie feel excited about school.

Step Three: What are all the solutions to the problem? Martha recommends that she talk to Suzie and see if she might discover an incident in the classroom that triggered the situation. Joan offers to think over the past week or two for changes that have occurred at home or otherwise.

Step Four: What is the best solution? Joan and Martha agree to visit by phone the next day with any additional information they might discover and check back every day until the situation is remedied.

Step Five: Check back: Is it working? Martha visits with Suzie and discovers that Suzie is upset because Martha took a piece of Suzie's artwork off the display board. Suzie thought the teacher didn't like her anymore because of it. After more questioning, Suzie's parents discover that several children had birthday celebrations the previous week. Since Suzie has a July birthday, she had not had a birthday celebration at school. Also, Suzie's mother had been gone the previous week for a two-day business trip.

After these findings, Joan and Martha plan a half-year birthday celebration for Suzie. Suzie's teacher makes a special effort to make Suzie feel included by adding a new piece of her work to the display board.

In a few days, with the cooperation of her parents and teacher, Suzie is back to her sunny self.

Work together

Unfortunately, too many times parents and teachers can overreact to a child's distress and not work together to bring about a happy solution. I've seen children removed from a school for problems similar to Suzie's because the parents or teachers lacked the problem-solving tools to effectively work through basic issues together. What a shame.

Use five-step problem solving with your children

This model of problem solving can also help our children learn critical thinking skills. Use this problem-solving technique with your child. You will be amazed at how well a three- or four-year-old can be stepped through this process. It is heartwarming to see a five-year-old use it with no adult guidance!

Three Keys to Optimizing Montessori Education

By understanding the relationships between freedom and choice and freedom and learning, you can effectively support your child's education. By looking at the big picture of your child's education, you'll be able to make superior decisions and commitments about your child's schooling. And lastly, realize that your child, your child's school, and your family are part of the world. There will be problems. Make sure you have the right people on your lifeboat and the tools and skills to work through problems.

In *Chapter 9, Seeing from a Child's Point of View,* we'll look at some perspectives that can help us better understand our children.

CHAPTER SUMMARY

When parents understand these three concepts I have found that their children are successful in Montessori learning environments.

1. As parents we need to understand the idea of free choice and how that relates to the growth of the human being, not only in children but also in adults.

2. When we can see the big picture of our child's development over a life-time of choices, we can be more confident of our decisions.

3. Life is problems and when we know how to deal head-on with problems we create successful situations.

Chapter 9

Seeing from a Child's Point of View

Becoming a Montessori Parent

One of my unusual gifts is that I have vivid memories from before I was two years old. It wasn't until I became a parent that it became a tool that I could use. It's not very cool to be fourteen and say, "Hey, I can remember what I did when I was two."

As a parent and as a teacher, I've appreciated this gift because it has helped me see the world from a child's eyes and understand almost intuitively how to help children.

When I started to write my newspaper column, "Kids Talk," I again drew on this gift to help communicate what I thought children would want us as adults to know, if only the children had the experience, the language, and the maturity to verbalize it.

At a Seattle Montessori conference in 2006, David Kahn, executive director for the North American Montessori Teachers Association (NAMTA), gave a talk entitled, "Ten Montessori Ideas That Convert Parents to the Child's Point of View."

David's presentation inspired me to take those ideas and turn them into columns, which I incorporate into this chapter.

Looking at these areas from the child's perspective can help make all of us into better parents.

Ten Points of View We Should Consider:
- The Child's Love of the Adult
- The Child's Love of their Environment
- The Child Is on a Continuous Path of Development
- The Child's Activities Reflect Sensitive Periods of Development
- The Child Develops by Activity
- The Child's Normal Development Requires Focused Activity
- The Child's Imagination Is Formed by Accurate Information
- The Child Is a Natural Born Optimist
- The Child Loves the Natural World
- The Child Is a Spiritual Embryo

View 1. The Child's Love of the Adult

Children are born with an ability to attach positively to the people and objects in their environments. That is why we have twenty-five-year-olds who still sleep with their childhood teddy bear. That is why, no matter what awful things a parent does, a child still wants to make him or her happy and seeks the parent's approval. Children have a tremendous capacity to love and be loved. As adults, we may too be busy to see it, and we may have forgotten those long-ago feelings and how we expressed them.

A child's natural love for the adult

In my kitchen at the back of the drawer that holds the hot pads is a green oven mitt. Worn, with a few holes in it, the mitt is visible every time I open the drawer. Its mate, regrettably, was lost in a move. The mitt's been around for over twenty years. It is my hope that it will always be there.

Mac's Hardware in Webster Groves in October of 1985 carried a little bit of everything—the usual nuts and bolts, children's toys and books, along with kitchen and gift items. For Dana, newly five, it was the place to buy her much-loved Mercer Mayer and Berenstain Bear books. Her recent birthday and allowances had created a bankroll of $12.50, enough to buy five of her favorite books.

For days Dana counted her money from her big pig bank, asking me if she had enough money for sales tax. She waited until Saturday to go to Mac's in order for her weekly allowance to be in hand.

Saturday morning arrived, and off we went to Mac's. As soon as we entered the store, Dana looked at me and said, "Mommy, you need to stay right here. I don't want you to help me. I want to buy this all by myself. Don't even look at the cash register."

I glanced at Dana then to our regular cashier, smiled, and nodded, promising to stay in gardening supplies. In a few minutes, the transaction was completed, and Dana grabbed my hand and said she was ready to go.

As she buckled her car seat, Dana held her bag tightly. Entering the house, Dana headed straight to her bedroom and shut the door. I figured she was eager to look at her birthday purchases.

The next morning at breakfast, Dana came downstairs holding a package wrapped in paper that she had designed and decorated.

A gift for me. As I opened the present, I gasped in surprise. Inside were two oven mitts. Forest green. I had admired them at the hardware store months before but had deemed them too expensive at $6.25 apiece. In 1985, you could eat a nice lunch out for $3.00, tip included.

Two oven mitts lay on my lap. Two mitts that took every penny my daughter had saved.

I had never been the recipient of such a gift.

"Do you like them, Mommy?"

"They," I said, "are the best gift ever."

In my kitchen drawer there is a worn, green oven mitt. For me, it symbolizes the love a child has for his or her parents. To me it represents how the love for adults, intense and pure, motivates the actions of children, if only we take the time to see from that point of view.

It is my hope the mitt will always be there, reminding me to evermore handle that love with care.

View 2. The Child's Love of their Environment

We are all born with a built-in love for our surroundings and the people included in those surroundings. Children give adults a powerful gift of their natural attachment and trust. As children we gave; now is our time to learn how to receive this precious present.

The child's love of place

"Education should be a social and human endeavor of interest to all." ~Maria Montessori

"We want to go see Ms. Maren," was the request of three of my former preschool students. Their mother, Pat, made arrangements for the boys to visit after school. The day arrived, and the boys came through the door, gave me a hug, then selected work off the classroom shelves. Pat and I visited over tea in the kitchen alcove. I waited for the boys to come "see" me, but they worked away and didn't say a word. Two hours passed, and it was time for them to leave.

"Thank you, Ms. Maren. I love you," each boy told me, but I felt a little like a girl who's been taken to the prom and never asked to dance. It didn't seem like the boys wanted to visit me at all.

The next day their father called and told me how much the boys had talked at dinner about visiting me. That was another time when I discovered the child's point of view. To a child, the adult in the environment and the environment are perceived as one and the same. To the boys, I was my classroom, and every activity in the classroom was me.

The child's love of the adults in his or her life extends to the surroundings that include those adults. We are given, just by being present, our children's love and trust. Children, by nature of being human, love and trust the adults in their lives and everything around those adults. Being at grandma's feels a lot like being with grandma.

It is this encompassing love that allows us as parents and grandparents to be powerful teachers, even if we are unaware the children are learning from us. For those of us who choose to teach, we need to be fully aware of this magnificent gift of love the child offers us.

On summer days, the music from the neighborhood ice cream truck brings back memories of my childhood: long shadows in the afternoon sun, the blue Oklahoma sky filled with cotton candy cumulus clouds, the scent of the mimosa tree, the houses across the street, my father's aqua 1958 Fiat in the driveway.

Because these memories were created by a child's intense love of place, or the love that surrounds family, they are vivid and fresh. As an extension of the love I have for my family, these remembrances remain intact after nearly fifty years.

All of us, from the driver of the ice cream truck to a neighbor a block away, create a child's sense of place, a place where love will be directed, attention will be focused, and life will be lived.

Each of us plays a vital role, whether we are aware of it or not, in creating a child's love of the world. The part we play in a child's life, conscious or unconscious, large or small, should compel us to be the best we can be.

View 3. The Child Is on a Continuous Path of Development

Each part of our path as a human being builds on the preceding periods of psychological and physical development. Humans are in the process of becoming adults from the moment of conception. Our children are traveling quickly through the four planes of development with significant changes occurring in predictable three- and six-year cycles.

Montessori philosophy and principles give us a road map to see where our children are headed and how we can be of service to their journey.

The child is always becoming

Whether we know it or not, each of us is on a continuum of

growth. Not being open to growth and change, though, can make us falter on our journey through life.

We all know people who have eddied out of the flow of life. They appear stuck in a routine and can't seem to find a way out.

Other folks seem to thrash around, caught in dramatic currents and undertows of life, struggling and expending great effort for little or no result.

When we are open to growth and learning, we become childlike again, enjoying the excitement and exhilaration of change, moving past obstacles.

"When I'm in fifth grade, I'll be as cool as Andrea," I thought as I stared out the bus window.

Andrea was a fifth grader when I was in third grade. Andrea was energetic, athletic, confident, and tan and lived a few blocks away. I searched for opportunities to watch her.

In our neighborhood of over fifty kids, Andrea rode her bike with an air of authority. She skated backwards down the street, turning effortlessly in circles. Andrea laughed easily, whistled two-fingered with earsplitting precision, and was surrounded by friends. Andrea was my vision of Nancy Drew as a ten-year-old.

As I swung my pigeon-toed, orthopedic-shoed feet on the bus, I dreamed of becoming—becoming someone like Andrea, not the shy, self-conscious, awkward bookworm that I was.

Summer vacation gave the neighborhood kids opportunities to roam the woods and creek in groups of two or three.

One day, my group came across Andrea's group in the creek bottom. "Come on," Andrea said. "I'll show you a place where we can swing across the creek like Tarzan."

We hiked what seemed like an hour to a part of the creek I'd never seen. Thick muscadine vines dangled from high, dark oak branches.

I was in heaven—an adventure with Andrea—even if I was breaking my mother's stay-within-earshot rule.

Andrea grabbed a vine, ran backwards, and swung easily to the opposite bank. Every girl sailed across multiple times as I watched.

"You can do it," Andrea yelled across the water. I was paralyzed. "We're leaving. Come on."

Rest of the girls walked ahead. "Run and go and hang on tight," Andrea shouted as she landed at my side.

I grabbed the grapevine, which was twice as thick as a baseball bat, walked backwards, and ran. For a few seconds, my arms burned as they held my body in space. My landing was not pretty. But Andrea was there, smiling.

As I stood up, my school bus daydreams became blazing potentialities. With dirty, bleeding knees, somehow I knew that I could become the person I wanted to be. I could change.

In those flying seconds, I saw that each of us has a vision of whom we could be, should be, and would be, if only we remain open to the possibilities that appear before us every day.

Every child is on a path of becoming. Developing a habit of becoming creates a way for us to remain open to a lifetime of opportunities and growth. Let us always remain open to the challenge of change. Let us guide children over the bumps, the ups, and the downs, as we all venture on this journey called life.

Run, go, and hang on tight.

View 4. The Child's Activities Reflect Sensitive Periods of Development

By observing children's activities, Montessori discovered that children at certain ages are drawn to specific actions due to the influence of sensitive periods of development and natural human tendencies toward behavior. During the first six years of life, children are attracted to activities that involve learning language, movement, refining the senses, order, and personal relationships.

The child has time-sensitive opportunities for growth

"No."

If we could have one word to associate with a two-year-old, it would be the word no.

When a two-year-old realizes that he or she has the power to decide by saying a simple yes or no, we can observe a time-sensitive period in a child's development. Establishing independence around age two and exerting a self-directed will are inherent growth patterns in all of us.

We can expect two-year-olds to express their will both verbally and physically. This expression is part of the natural human process of realizing that you are an individual with particular needs. Around age six, children begin to develop a sense of belonging to a group and become aware that the group has specific needs and desires outside each individual. Until that juncture in development, it is unrealistic for us to expect a child to understand others' needs.

There are natural times in a person's life that learning about how to become an individual, how to walk, how to talk, and how to become part of a group are part of the innate process of human development. When a person fails to acquire certain skills at these important times, the effects can have long-term significance.

We know that if a child doesn't speak a language by the age of six, the chances are the child will never be fluent in any language. This is due to a sensitive period of language development in children from birth to the age of six.

Before the age of six, children are in a period of growth where learning appears effortless. The child absorbs information and learns from interactions with the world. We don't have to teach a child how to walk or talk because of these instinctive periods of development for language and movement.

Through their sixth year, children are in five critical developmental periods. We can support this time of learning by being aware that this developmental growth is driving children's behavior. As we watch our children, we can see that they are attracted to activities in these five areas:

- Language
- Movement
- Sensory perception
- Understanding of the order of people, places, and things

- Developing social skills and relationships

Children are drawn to activities that help them create language, both spoken and written. They are acquiring motor skills, both large and small, and have a need to be involved in actions that use their whole body and/or hands. Hand and eye coordination is developing along with the senses of taste, smell, and touch. Understanding what noises to pay attention to is also part of children's normal process. For example, the child is learning to discern which is more important, the voices on the television or the adults in the room.

Understanding the order to everyday life, the significance of people in the child's life, and the physical order of the world around him or her guides the child's behavior, and a disruption in that perceived order could create disturbances in the child's behavior.

The child is interested in how to interact with others and easily learns a multitude of socials skills such as please and thank you. The child is also creating a foundation for interpersonal relationships while learning how to interact with family and close friends.

These five time-sensitive areas for learning in the child create a driving force for the child's actions, demeanor, and conduct. When you can recognize these forces of development within the child, you can be of genuine assistance as the child creates his or her unique personality and an individual who contributes to the whole of life.

View 5. The Child Develops by Activity

When we can watch children through the lenses of sensitive periods and human tendencies, we can focus on the developmental continuum our children are traveling and predict the outcomes of the activities in which our children are involved.

Understanding the child's attraction to certain activities can help us keep a certain perspective and a sense of humor about being a parent.

A child's actions are development-driven

"What's that? What's that?" two-year-old Joshua asked about every new person, place, item, or sound encountered on a shopping excursion. Tim and Marcy, Joshua's parents, began to realize that their chances for a conversation or a cup of coffee on this outing were futile. Joshua's behavior made it truly out of the question.

Joshua fussed to get out of his stroller, and as soon as he was free to walk, he ran towards items of interest. As soon as his "What's that?" question was answered, off he went in another direction in pursuit of the next novel experience. Trying to keep up with Joshua exhausted Tim and Marcy.

As we watch our children, we can see that they are attracted to activities in these five areas: language; movement; sensory perception; understanding of the order of people, places, and things; and developing social skills and relationships.

These five time-sensitive areas for learning in the child create a driving force for the child's actions, demeanor, and conduct. When we can recognize these forces of development within the child, we can be of genuine assistance as the child creates his or her unique personality and grows into an individual who contributes to the whole.

When we consider Joshua's behavior by looking at these five sensitive periods of learning for the child between birth and age six, we begin to see how a child's actions are based on these distinct developmental needs.

With Joshua's "What's that?" question, we can see his need to learn new vocabulary while understanding the order of these new items and how they relate to his previous experiences. Joshua frequently would continue asking "What's that?" until a color was named, thus helping him learn the words for various colors. Joshua had a need to move as he ran to see new things. Being a quiet observer was not part of Joshua's learning style. Joshua's shopping trip helped broaden his social experience as well as strengthen his relationship with his parents as he learned to trust their input.

Frustrated and tired after this shopping expedition with Joshua, Tim and Marcy had almost decided not to take Joshua on any more outings. When they discovered that Joshua's behavior was driven by his natural development to acquire critical skills, Tim and Marcy took a fresh approach to family excursions.

Instead of trying to include Joshua on their errands, Marcy and Tim decided to design outings that would focus on Joshua's need to have experiences that aided language, movement, sensory skills, social development, and understanding the order of the world. Tim and Marcy, instead of being impatient with what could be seen as Joshua's demands, refocused on Joshua's conduct as exploration necessary for him to build new skills.

Tim and Marcy learned to see situations from the viewpoint of a child, a child unconsciously trying to create his unique personality. This perspective helped Tim and Marcy anticipate Joshua's behavior in various situations. When they saw Joshua's behavior as a way to meet his learning needs, family outings became fun for everyone. On the outings when they found time to sip a latte, Tim and Marcy enjoyed discussing Joshua's progress instead of complaining about his behavior.

View 6. The Child's Normal Development Requires Focused Activity

The process of normalization, or normal development, is characterized by four attributes:
- A love of work or activity
- Concentration on an activity
- Self-discipline (focused attention)
- Sociability or joyful work

Humans, whatever age, are seeking activities that fully engage them, absorb them, and in the process create a sense of inner satisfaction that is seen in an outward manifestation of joy and friendship.

We all want to whistle while we work, and when we are finished working, we want the satisfaction of a job well done to share with others.

Children seek to create a flow of activity

Up. Down. Up. Down. Eight-month-old Dana stood holding onto the coffee table doing deep knee bends, day after day, over two hundred at a time, perhaps thousands a day.

In amazement, I watched as Dana tirelessly exercised. There was no way I could do a thousand deep knee bends in a day and still be able to get out of bed the next day.

Mentioning Dana's gymnastics to my mother, she told me, "It won't be long before she walks."

Mom was right. Dana was walking within two weeks.

Young children repeat an activity over and over again for several reasons: to perfect the movement, to create learning and knowledge within that activity, or to gain a natural high or "in the zone" feeling of perfecting a challenging skill.

When given the opportunity to repeat self-selected activities, children under the age of six will do so until there is some inner satisfaction of accomplishment.

Mihaly Csikszentmihalyi, in his book, *Finding Flow: The Psychology of Engagement with Everyday Life,* refers to this repetition of a challenging activity as being in "flow." True learning occurs at all ages as we grasp a new skill or concept and then repeat the experience—be it riding a bike or doing a division problem. Learning occurs at that moment when we finally "get it" and can repeat an activity independently.

As we get older, starting at around age six, we continue to create moments of deep satisfaction through learning new activities but require a novel twist to create the challenge that will put us back in the zone.

The key to learning for the older child and for the adult is to present activities with an added twist or challenge, building upon previous learning while creating a satisfying flow of activity. For example, perhaps we start to learn to shoot baskets with the hoop lowered. Little by little, we raise the hoop to standard height. We might begin shooting free throws in front of the line, stepping back day-by-day until we can shoot from the line. Adding challenge incrementally and spicing things up by using different methods keeps us in a flow of activity that makes learning a new skill exciting and rewarding.

As adults, we are responsible for challenging ourselves. As we become more responsible and self-directed in our learning and personal growth, we need to remain committed to personal development and learning. Not being able to focus on new or challenging experiences to create a flow of activity causes us to become bored, depressed, and discontented.

Young children show us the way to create a pattern of challenging growth for a lifetime. That template looks something like this:

1. Choose an activity.
2. Repeat it until you "get it" and can do it easily.
3. Once you master an activity, repeat it often in order to solidify learning and create the "flow zone" for learning.
4. To create new learning, add variety and challenges to mastered skills.
5. The more time you spend in zone, the more apt you are to have the confidence to take on larger or more difficult situations.

Athletes such as runners experience being in the zone or in flow usually after only twenty minutes of activity. To add to their personal best, athletes challenge themselves by trying to go faster, longer, stronger, or higher than before. Understanding that repeated activity leads to learning and self-satisfaction helped an athletic shoe company pick their slogan of "Just Do It." That's a good way to learn and enlarge our experiences: we just have to do it.

As you watch your youngster repeat activities, remember that this is how we learn. The successful repetition of challenging activities is the way our children lay a foundation for a lifetime of fun-filled learning.

View 7. The Child's Imagination Is Formed by Accurate Information

Learning in the child older than six years is fueled by the imagination, the mind's ability to see something that is not right in front of you. But to be able to fully utilize the imagination and its ability to be creative, the mind requires accurate sensory information during the first six years of life.

When we as parents can understand the child's view on what the mind needs, creating meaningful experiences becomes easier.

Imagination in the young child

Imagination is the ability to visualize something that is not physically present.

Infants have little if any imagination. If the familiar is gone, distress and tears usually follow. A new situation, such as being left alone, can be painful to the child until the child learns that this situation is safe or parents return.

Experiences, positive and negative, create a certain level of expectation in the young child. The child is learning: If I'm hungry, will there be food? If I'm tired, will I be able to rest peacefully? If I'm wet and uncomfortable, will someone come and change me? Experiences create what the child can visualize with objects not being in sight.

As a child's basic needs are met or not met as the case may be, the child learns to picture things that are not with him or her. The child learns that food appears when he cries, at predictable times, or haphazardly. As physical needs are met, the toddler begins to learn to imagine.

Imagination in the child under age six is experience-driven. To help the child build correct images of the world in his or her mind, reality and language content around those experiences need to be accurate.

We can be of great assistance to the young child by giving him or her fact- and reality-based experiences involving all the senses-- seeing, hearing, touching, tasting, and smelling.

Until about age six or seven, the child is in a sensitive period of growth for taking in information. The child's mind perceives every event as real. For example, the emotional and mental impact of seeing violence on television or video games affects the child's brain as if the incident had occurred right in front of the child. The young child's mind cannot differentiate between real and make-believe. A murder on the TV screen is perceived as real.

The young child needs a diet of accurate information and facts to form a foundation for the later developing imagination. Beginning in a child's sixth year, learning is fueled by the imagination. As adults, we must draw on our imaginations to decide the life we want to live. This sensorial foundation for imagination in the young child needs to be protected and nurtured.

We need to protect the child from violence and hostile images. We should use the right word for objects in the child's environment. Water is not "wa-wa." A rubber duck is not a "duckie-poo." With our movements and our words, we model acceptable behavior.

We can nurture the imagination with a fun and simple game called "What's Missing?" To play, gather six to ten small items: for example, a comb, a pencil, a fork, a spoon, a clothespin, and an eraser. Name each item with the children so they will know the correct name. Ask the children to turn around or hide their eyes for ten seconds by counting to ten. For an added challenge, count in another language, or lengthen attention by counting to twenty or thirty.

While the children are looking away, take one item and hide it behind your back. Ask, "What's missing?"

If the children have difficulty, bring the item out and say, "The comb was missing. Let's do another object."

Most children from age two and a half to six years love this game and will play everyday for months with a variety of items. Increase the number of items every few days or take multiple items away to increase the level of difficulty. Kit Carson, the legendary frontiersman, purportedly could recall a hundred items after viewing them for one minute. That's one skill of an imagining mind.

A vivid and accurate imagination will help our children design and create a marvelous life with the resources they have available.

View 8. The Child is a Natural Born Optimist

Children are born with a natural propensity to connect in a positive way to life. Children are born to engage with love and enthusiasm. We might say that children are the source of love. Children create a type of positive psychology for us if we are only open to it.

The positive psychology of childhood

Children under the age of seven are in a developmental period for creating social relationships. Children want to connect and develop bonds of trust, respect, and love with the people around them. Children are designed to want to connect positively with the adults in their lives. Children are naturally motivated to love.

Unfortunately, the dynamics of relationship building for the child can be thwarted by obstacles created by the adults in the child's life. When children hit stumbling blocks to positive engagement, we may witness defiant behaviors, tantrums, and discouragement in the child.

When a child cannot constructively engage with parents or other adults, we may see the child act disobediently to get attention. If not redirected in a positive manner, the child may learn to ignore adults and become passive, resistant, or ambivalent about these relationships.

The child's innate tendency is to be involved in purposeful activity to help others. When a child is concentrating on an activity with positive connections to the people around him or her, we observe a happy and joyful child.

When we see a child behave in a way that is not constructive, we are almost assured that the child has lost a necessary and vital connection to the adults in his or her life. An unhappy child gives us a clue that the child has a problematic relationship to an essential adult.

When a child loses this supportive connection to an adult, the child's motivation and behavior is ruled by fear—fear of losing love and fear of losing the adults in his or her life. What we perceive as misbehavior is a child's cry for help and love.

If our efforts to connect to the child are not based on love and genuine concern and instead are based on our own fears—such as our children being an embarrassment to us—we will not be able to reconnect and use the inborn positive psychology of the child.

If we yell at or punish our children in attempts to change their behavior, our yelling and punishments should be a signal to us to change our behavior. When we find ourselves choosing to "do to" our children instead of "work with" our children, we need to realize we have lost contact with our children's love, respect, and trust.

When a child feels disconnected from his or her parents, the child goes through three stages of emotional reactions. First is protest, in which the child cries and refuses to be consoled by others. Second is despair, in which the child is sad and passive. Third is detachment, in which the child actively disregards the parent.

To reconnect to the positive psychology of the child, we must strive to see the child's innate love, respect, and trust for others and how those qualities motivate behavior.

We must consider what actions, words, or physical barriers keep the child from expressing or experiencing our love. We need to watch for situations that create emotional reactions in the child of protest, passivity, or disregard. A misbehaving child is a discouraged child who does not feel joined to the ones he or she loves.

Do we respect the child's efforts and rights? We need to listen to our children and take their point of view seriously and respectfully. Respect can help us reconnect.

Do we act in such a manner to always instill trust in our relationship with the child? We need to encourage our children to talk to us so that we will know what we are doing right, where we need to improve, and how we might change. Even a two-year-old can give us valuable feedback on how our actions are, or are not, establishing a trusting relationship.

Children are instinctively predisposed to want to connect in a constructive, loving way. Children's behavior lets us know if they feel connected to us or not. Use the child's innate positive psychology to create a lifelong bond of love, trust, and respect.

View 9. The Child Loves the Natural World

Several years ago I read a book of stories of how people had risen to the top of their professional lives.

One story that has stayed with me, and I think of it every time I look at the stars, is the story of an astronomer.

This scientist was raised in New York City until the age of five when her parents bought a house out in the suburbs. They arrived at their new home on a clear, dark night. As her father carried her into the house, she looked up and saw the stars for the first time in her life. She refused to go into the house, and her parents stayed outdoors with her the rest of the night, gazing at the stars.

That night, in her father's arms, she began a love affair with the stars that has never stopped. The child in all of us, given clear vision, stands in adoration of our universe.

The child's inherent love of nature

What do you do to find yourself when you are out of sorts? Frustrated? Sorrowful? Despairing?

If you are like many people, you try to find a quiet spot to commune with nature and seek peace or solace. Solace is a word from the Latin word solari meaning to console or comfort. The Latin sol or sun, forms the word solace. We have to be close to nature to find the solace of the sun, and in the process we find ourselves.

This connection to peace is formed within each of us as a young child. Humans are born with an innate ability to constructively connect to the world around us using all our senses--seeing, hearing, touching, smelling, and tasting. As infants, we attach ourselves lovingly to items that we see, touch, taste, hear, and smell. Think of all the blankets and stuffed toys in the world, doted on for years by their small owners. As every parent knows after a bleary-eyed midnight search for a lost "blankie," a misplaced object of affection can create inconsolable anguish in a child.

Wherever we go in the world, even when security blankets and stuffed animals are left behind, nature is there to comfort us. The sun, the moon, and the stars belong to us forever. The wind, the smell of rain, the feel of rocks, dirt, and sand, the rustle of trees, the colors of flowers, the shifting forms of clouds, the prickle of grass between our toes—are there wherever we go. The call of a bird, an earthworm, or a squirrel running up a tree can help us connect to that peaceful part of us.

These childhood connections to nature remain strong throughout all of our lives.

On a trip to pick apples, my husband called his mother to ask if we could bring her apples. "I'd love to have some King apples," she said. "We had a King apple tree in our yard when I was a kid." Her first choice of apples was the kind that grew in her backyard when she was a five-year-old.

We are meant to connect to our time and place through our love of nature. This connection to the earth creates a way for us to remember who we are and that the beauty of the universe belongs to every one of us on this planet. All we have to do is be.

Even though I have been alive for over eighteen thousand sunsets, my favorites are the red/purple/pink big sky ones of my Oklahoma childhood. There is something indescribably comforting to me in those bold water-colored sunsets.

This love of nature formed in childhood, from apples to sunsets, gives our soul roots. From these roots we sprout wings, carrying us on the adventure of our life.

Have you taken a child on a walk today? Taste the rain, smell the sun, hear the trees, watch the wind, and touch a heart.

View 10. The Child Is a Spiritual Embryo

Human beings can be wonderfully resilient. This resiliency is due to the strength of the human spirit. It is the role of family to protect and nurture the spirit of the child where the seeds of human greatness germinate.

The spiritual role of family

To our children, we are their first experience of the divine, the all-powerful, the all-knowing, with a human face. We fix ZuZu's petals. We are our children's miracle makers.

Our ability to create can be a double-edged sword by yielding the power to destroy or obstruct our children's development.

Our children come to us as spiritual embryos, beings working to build themselves. From birth, children have an inner life. Human development is a lengthy and internal process—an enigma that produces unpredictable results.

The problem with human development is the fact that the child has a spiritual life, even when he or she cannot express it. Because of the arduousness of this development, growth occurs over a long period of time. A child usually learns to walk by eighteen months of age. The effort the child uses to learn to walk is small compared to the internal work of the spirit.

A spirit is born, hidden in a small body, who little by little learns to exert his or her will in the world. The largest obstacle and the greatest help in the child's new world is the adult who has enormous power, power that is too frequently not fully understood or exercised.

Like the physical body, the spiritual embryo must be protected in an environment filled with the richness of love and respect for the development of the child.

As the adults, we have three principles that we should follow to protect the spirit of the child:

1. Respect all reasonable forms of activity in which the child engages and try to understand those activities.
2. Support as much as possible the child's desires for activity. This doesn't mean that we wait on the child hand and foot,

but we encourage activity in order to draw out the child's singular and independent spirit.

3. Be careful in our relationships with children because they are more sensitive than we know.

I'm reminded of the movie *E.T.* where three children discover an extraterrestrial. The children are careful to help E.T. meet his needs and protect him from the adults who would capture, examine, and overanalyze him to death.

Let us observe children's activities and realize that these activities are the manifestations of the spirit within. Our children's activities are clues to their inner workings of spirit. Our children need our help to create an environment in which their spiritual embryos can grow stronger and healthier day by day.

As we observe our children, let us realize that tears, screams, misbehavior, shyness, disobedience, lying, egoism, and destructiveness are defense mechanisms of the child. These behaviors are attempts to gain our help to remove an obstruction to growth.

Children come to us very much as extraterrestrials. We need to remember that children are new souls to this planet. Let us strive to be sensitive to our children's needs, both physical and spiritual.

CHAPTER SUMMARY

Our children have a huge task before them, the task of becoming an adult human being. Parents also have an immense challenge. We need to be a help to life. To be a help to our children's lives we must first see clearly what needs to be accomplished.

When we fail to consider the child's perspective of life, we may hold unrealistic expectations about our children and become frustrated as parents. Seeing from the child's point of view creates an understanding of children that can bring us great joy as parents for all of our lives.

Syd Kruse

Chapter 10

Montessori Vocabulary Made Clear

Every discipline has its specific jargon. Lawyers, doctors, car mechanics, computer technicians, gardeners, and gymnasts each have terms that are unique to their area of expertise.

So it is with Montessori work. We want you to have a handy reference for the language that is used in Montessori books, classrooms and schools.

We hope this vocabulary guide will help you feel comfortable with the Montessori specific words in this book, in your child's school, and in Dr. Montessori's books. Also, if there is some idea or concept you don't understand, please visit with your child's teacher or school administrator. They are in a "sensitive period" for helping parents.

Absorbent Mind: Dr. Montessori used the term absorbent mind to express the concept of education being a "natural process which develops spontaneously in the human being." The absorbent mind is a "special psychic force at work, helping the little child to develop" (*The Absorbent Mind*, pages 6–7).

This natural power that children possess helps them absorb and learn from the world around them.

Activity Charts: Montessori teacher trainers recommend that teachers keep observation charts or activity charts on their students. The charts indicate the child's work during a three-hour-work-cycle and the levels of concentration observed by the Montessori teacher.

Administration: Smaller schools tend to have teaching directors who are committed to an authentic Montessori experience. As schools grow larger, the administrative duties also enlarge, and schools may elect to hire professional managers. In public school settings, district or state policy may require school directors to have certain credentials, such as a graduate degree in public administration. It is critical for a Montessori school administrator to have a thorough knowledge of Montessori philosophy, to understand the needs of children, and to have a commitment to an authentic Montessori program.

Be sure to ask about the Montessori credentials and experience of both teachers and administrators as you look at schools.

Adolescence: Adolescence refers to the ages of twelve to eighteen years. There are two sub-stages of development during this time, twelve to fifteen and fifteen to eighteen, with each sub-stage having different learning requirements and environments distinct from elementary and each other. Read more about adolescence in Chapter 4.

Albums: During Montessori teacher training, trainees create teaching albums they will use as teachers. These notebooks contain lessons they will teach. Depending on the type and level of training, a teacher may have six to twelve albums containing hundreds of illustrated lessons they have learned to give. Part of the teacher certification process is to make sure that these albums are complete and precise. The teacher is also given an oral test to make sure he or she is competent with these lessons.

Analysis of Movement: As Montessori teachers observe a child at work having difficulties, they will analyze the movements necessary for success in that activity. Each movement will be introduced either directly or indirectly to assure the child's success in that activity.

For example, if a child is having difficulty opening a jar, the teacher may indirectly work on strengthening the arm with polishing lessons or directly work on the skills by offering a lesson with various types of jars to be opened.

Apparatus: The word apparatus is used interchangeably with the terms Montessori materials and didactic materials.

Assistant: Montessori classrooms may have a paraprofessional assistant who commonly is trained in-house for the role of classroom assistant.

Authentic Montessori: Due to the proliferation of many types of Montessori teacher training and school implementation, the concept of "authentic Montessori" has come to the forefront over the past twenty years.

There are many types of schools and teachers that claim to be "Montessori", and any school can say they are a Montessori school. Authentic Montessori schools share these three vital characteristics:

1. Adults professionally trained in Montessori philosophy, methods and materials for the group they are teaching
2. Prepared environments based on three-year age groups
3. Children's free choice of activity within a three-hour work cycle.

Without these essential components a Montessori school might be a "Monte-something" school, not offering a rich Montessori school experience. In *Chapter 6, Finding a Quality Montessori School*, we'll show you how to find authentic Montessori programs.

Auto-Education: The idea of auto-education is linked with the concept of self-construction in Montessori philosophy, and some people view it as the same idea. There is a nuance though that with auto-education a person consciously takes responsibility for his or her education. Self-construction has a connotation of activities, or work, being unconsciously performed by the child to build foundational skills before the age of six years.

Casa Dei Bambini: Casa, or "house" in Italian, refers to the environment for children ages three to six years. Dr. Montessori referred to the first schools as Casa Dei Bambini or Children's Houses.

See *Children's House.*

Children's House: Many schools use the term Children's House to refer to the classroom for children ages three to six years. Some schools may also refer to this age group as the Casa, preschool, early childhood, or primary group.

See *Casa dei bambini.*

Community: The term community is used in Montessori circles to mean the children, families, and staff of a classroom or school. For example, the infant-toddler community would include the children in that classroom, the children's families, along with teachers, assistants, and administrators.

Continuum of Development: Montessori educators understand the child is changing constantly along a path of human growth. At different stages of this course of development, the child will exhibit behaviors and have needs that are characteristic to that time of life or stage of development. Dr. Montessori referred to this continuum of development as the four planes of development.

Cosmic Education: Dr. Montessori saw the use of the imagination as the key to learning for children ages six to twelve years of age. Montessori urged us to give the child a "vision of the universe" because within this view there would be something that would fire each individual child's imagination and something that would draw the child's interest. As the child pursues areas of interest, all subjects of learning are touched upon due to the interconnectedness of everything in the cosmos.

John Muir understood cosmic education when he wrote, "When one tugs at a single thing in nature he finds it attached to the rest of the world."

With cosmic education we try to help the child find that thing to tug, and the marvels of the universe begin to unfold.

Dr. Montessori may have preferred to use the term "universal education," but that phrase was already in use in the United States at the time, relating to educator John Dewey's idea of free public education for everyone.

Instead, the term cosmic education, or connecting the child to the idea of the universe or cosmos, was used. Back in the 1970s and '80s, the term seemed a bit "out there" for mainstream use. Now there is more of a cultural awareness that everything is indeed connected to everything else, and the term cosmic education seems to better communicate the idea of giving the child a vision of the whole, or the cosmos.

Deviations: During the course of normal human development, all of us get bumped off course or take deviations. Dr. Montessori described two types of detours: fugues and barriers. *Fugues* refer to flights of fantasy and taking refuge from perceived difficulty or danger. *Barriers* involve the child drawing into him or herself and erecting psychic "walls" against certain types of experiences.

A child returns to normal development, and away from developmental detours, when he or she can concentrate on a physical activity that connects him or her to the exterior world in meaningful ways. The child's focused activity is the healing agent that returns the child to normal and natural development.

Didactic Materials: See *Montessori Materials.*

Directress or Director: See *Montessori Teacher*.

Elementary Community: The elementary community is comprised of all the children, teachers, parents, and adults in a school's elementary classrooms or environments. As community relationships are established, other people involved in strategic relationships with the school—such as museum docents, librarians, storekeepers, and master gardeners—are considered part of the community.

Elementary Environment: The elementary environment is designed for children ages six to twelve years. There may be a lower elementary made up of six- to nine-year-olds and an upper elementary comprised of nine- to twelve-year-olds. Elementary classrooms for six- to twelve-year-olds are also common. The elementary environment includes an outdoor component but also expands to encompass the children "going out" to explore their local community's museums, libraries, and other facilities outside of the school campus.

Enlightened Adults: Dr. Montessori had in mind that children should have adults around them who understand children's developmental needs and are in "humble service to the child." Enlightened adults serve the child and can imagine the adult who is not yet there.

Environment: The term environment in Montessori terms is used to describe a prepared environment that meets the learning needs of the age group it serves.

You will hear the word environment and classroom used interchangeably. A Montessori classroom or environment does not look anything like a traditional classroom. A primary environment for three- to six-years-olds is different than an elementary environment, which differs from an adolescent environment.

Erdkinder: Dr. Montessori envisioned an Erdkinder (German for "child of the earth") environment for the young adolescent, ages twelve to fifteen years, to fulfill a developmental need to connect to nature and form a society of his or her time and place. This vision of Erdkinder encompasses the idea of a working farm and much more. For the past ten years, this Montessori farm school concept, or Erdkinder, has been successfully implemented in the United States.

Four Planes of Development: Dr. Montessori saw the human being going through four planes, or stages, of development with each plane having unique characteristics and opportunities for learning.

First Plane:	From birth to six years,
Second Plane:	From six to twelve years,
Third Plane:	From twelve to eighteen years, and
Fourth Plane:	From eighteen to twenty-four years

Free Choice: When we give our children choices, we are helping them become good decision makers, and we help them bring a powerful force of will to their learning. Free choice is not about doing what we like, but liking what we do. Free choice is not about indulging idle curiosity; it is about allowing the child to choose to develop skills and deepen knowledge in an activity that has been introduced. This free choice allows the child to bring an enthusiasm to learning that might be extinguished under force.

Freedom and Responsibility: The idea that freedom follows responsible behavior is an important concept in Montessori philosophy. We give opportunities to "respond with ability" and corresponding freedoms are given. For example, if you remember to bring your coat, then you will be given the freedom to go outside when it is cold. If you act responsibly in the elementary classroom, then you can be granted the freedom to go outside of the classroom into the larger community. See *Going Out.*

Freedom within Limits: The concept of allowing freedom within limits is a crucial idea in Montessori philosophy. To the casual observer or new teacher, freedom may appear to allow a child to do anything he or she would like.

Freedom is limited by the level of ability and responsibility a child has. We give the child the freedom to move freely about the classroom. This freedom may be taken away if the child uses the freedom to hit other children, to disrupt others' work, to damage materials, or otherwise to not choose a purposeful activity. The child is free to act within the limits of purposeful activity.

Going Out: The idea of going out is very different than the typical field trip that traditional elementary students take. Students in a Montessori elementary classroom will go out in small groups of two to perhaps six students into the community to gather information or experiences in areas of interest. For example, some schools are able to let students walk a few blocks to the city library. Other schools allow students to take public transportation to go to museums or college campuses to visit with experts in their field of study. Others have a system of parent volunteers who drive and chaperone students going out.

A going out program is possible due to the child developing freedom and responsibility over a period of many years. Students must earn the right to go out.

Grace and Courtesy: The lessons in grace and courtesy are designed to build vital social skills. From the basics of saying please and thank you to learning how to politely interrupt a conversation, how to ask for assistance, how to greet a guest, and many more, your child is introduced to foundational skills for a lifetime of healthy relationships.

Guide or Guido: See *Montessori Teacher*.

Horme: Dr. Montessori used this psychological term from Sir Percy Nunn. Horme means life force (from the Greek horme, meaning "impetus or impulse").

If the life force is allowed to flow smoothly without obstacles impairing its power, normalization, meaning natural development, occurs. When the horme is blocked, we see detours in the life force, and the process of normalization does not occur. If the hormic force is strong and diverted from the path of normal development, we may see a child with powerful emotional and physical outbursts. If the horme is weak in a child, we may observe boredom, laziness, and the need to be constantly entertained.

Human Tendencies: Dr. Montessori saw that there were certain characteristics that make us human. Depending on our individual natures, sensitive periods of learning, or different psychological characteristics, the following activities define us as human. At various points in human development, certain tendencies appear stronger.

These tendencies include: activity, becoming, belonging, exploration, orientation, order, communication, imagination, exactness, repetition, and perfection.

Human beings need to be involved in meaningful activities. They need to feel a sense of becoming. Humans need to belong. They need to explore the world around them and create an orientation for that exploration. People have a need to create order and make sense out of the chaos around them. We need to communicate with others. We use our imaginations. We work at exactness. We learn using repetition. We yearn for perfection.

Human tendencies and human needs drive human behavior. Montessori pedagogical principles use and are based on the knowledge of the human tendencies.

Independence and Concentration: As we observe the child at work doing meaningful activities, Montessorians look for developing independence and concentration in the child. These two qualities create the foundational skills necessary for future success.

For example, if a child shows independence and concentration by sweeping the floor at the age of three years, the child will bring that same independence and concentration to the more academic work of the four- and five-year-olds in a Montessori classroom.

Infant-Toddler: Infant-toddler refers to the age span from birth to around age three. The infant-toddler communities are divided into two areas—the Nido for ages two to fourteen months and the young children's communities for children ages fourteen to thirty-six months.

Not every Montessori school offers an infant-toddler program. Many infant-toddler programs are self-contained and feed into schools that have students ages three to six years.

Inner Teacher: The child's self-construction is aided by what Montessorians call the inner teacher, or the child's unconscious urge to pursue certain activities. The outward manifestations of the child's inner teacher are the child's interest and attention. We encourage interest through the prepared environment and an awareness of our role in the work of the child.

For example, we observe a child's interest in music by observing his or her choice of playing the bells in the Montessori classroom. The child's inner teacher is urging the child to make music.

A trained Montessori teacher in a prepared environment helps guide the child to meaningful activities, thus aiding the child's self-construction.

Keys to the World: Dr. Montessori asked us to give the children in the primary classroom the keys to the world. By this she referred to the essential elements needed for understanding mathematics, language, reading, writing, and all other areas of human interest. For example, the keys to mathematics are the numerals of the decimal system; the constructs of units, tens, hundreds and thousands used in our decimal system; and the four basic arithmetic operations of addition, subtraction, multiplication and division. Another math key might be seen in the idea that we count linearly, one by one.

The Montessori materials and lessons hold the keys to the child's understanding of the world.

Lower Elementary: The elementary age group in many schools is divided into two classes, the lower and upper elementary. The lower elementary is for those children who show psychological characteristics of being in the second of the four planes of development.

Ages given for each plane of development are approximate and are used as guidelines to aid observation of the child's choices for work in order to know when the child is ready to enter a new learning environment. Montessori teachers are trained to offer key lessons to direct and encourage the child's areas of interest.

A child who is past his or her sixth birthday may or may not exhibit the psychological characteristics of the child in the second plane of development. Until these characteristics are observed, the child is best served by remaining in the primary environment of the Casa.

Mneme: Mneme was the Greek Muse for memory. Dr. Montessori used this psychological term to express the idea of memory being created and retained in the child through sensorial experiences.

Montessori: The term Montessori is used in several contexts and can be confusing. Montessori can refer to Dr. Maria Montessori as an individual, to Montessori education in general, or to Montessori philosophy, methods, and materials.

Montessorians: Montessorians refer to those people who try to implement Montessori principles in schools, homes and the larger world. Teachers, parents, school administrators, children's museum designer's and more call themselves Montessorians.

Montessori Materials: Montessori materials are a variety of hands-on lessons that are either manufactured or teacher made. These materials were designed and incorporated into the work with the children by Dr. Montessori, her son Mario, and original Montessori adherents.

Dr. Montessori used materials made by Itard and Seguin, notably the Moveable Alphabet and Command Cards from Itard and the Teens Board and Tens Board from Seguin. Other materials are designed to reveal certain concepts to the child through hands-on, uninterrupted exploration after an introductory lesson from the Montessori teacher.

For example, the Pink Tower contains multiple concepts, including height, volume, sequence, squares of numbers, and cubes of numbers, among other abstractions.

There are dozens of pieces of Montessori-designed materials that help the child in educating the senses of hearing, seeing, smelling, touching, and tasting. Other Montessori materials aid the child in acquiring skills in math, reading, writing, geography, social studies, science, music, and more. Each piece of material can be used in a variety of ways to illuminate various concepts.

A properly Montessori prepared environment should contain a full complement of Montessori materials.

Also see *sensorial materials.*

Montessori Teacher: A Montessori teacher has Montessori training in the age level at which he or she is teaching. There are trainings for Assistants to Infancy for working with children from birth to age three; primary training for working with children ages three to six; and elementary training for working with ages six to twelve. Adolescent training for working with twelve- to eighteen-year-olds is now being developed. Most adolescent teachers have elementary training with additional adolescent training.

A Montessori teacher is trained to observe children in a specific age group and introduce them to developmentally challenging activities based on those observations. A Montessori elementary teacher, for example, is trained to work with six- to twelve-year-olds and has fundamental versus specific knowledge of the work with the younger and older children. Primary teachers, likewise, have general knowledge of the work of the elementary-aged child but will not be trained to observe and give lessons to the elementary-aged child.

Many Montessorians prefer to use the term guide or director/directress instead of teacher to describe their work with the child. Dr. Montessori used the term guido in her writings. The Montessori teacher's job is to help direct or guide the child to purposeful activity. The Montessori guide directs the successful learning and developmental progress of children. This fundamental view of how to interact with the child is one of the major principles of Montessori philosophy. The adult's job is to prepare an environment in order to guide and direct the child to purposeful activity.

When I first became a Montessori-certified teacher, I proudly introduced myself as a Montessori guide at dinner parties, and people asked me to lead float trips down the Buffalo River. Even though the word "guide" communicates more clearly the role the adult plays in a Montessori classroom, I realize that most folks might think guide means river rafter.

The job of a Montessori guide is to help children learn. As a college professor of mine said, "I'm a Ph.D. in chemistry. My job is to present information. Your job is to learn it." Unfortunately, I've seen too many teachers over the years who see their job as presenting information with little concern if a student actually learns that information. The word "guide" to me connotes that you are committed to helping someone reach a destination.

I would rather be guided than taught. With a guide, I'll end up where I want to be.

Most Montessori schools use the word teacher out of a desire to communicate effectively with parents whose experience has primarily been with "teachers."

Montessori teachers are guides, and that is very good for your child.

Montessori Teacher Training: There are several training programs in the United States, the most well-known being Association Montessori Internationale (AMI) and American Montessori Society (AMS), as well as National Center for Montessori Education (NCME), which recently merged with AMS. Montessori Education Programs International and Southwest Montessori Training Center are also popular training programs. Distance learning programs are coming online such as the Center for Guided Montessori Studies (CGMS). The Montessori Accreditation Council for Teacher Education (MACTE) oversees

Montessori teacher training programs in the United States.

These Montessori teacher programs usually require a bachelor's degree for entrance and have rigorous requirements for showing proficiency in how to use the Montessori materials and in understanding the developmental needs of the children. Many Montessori training programs work in conjunction with a college and offer the option of a master's degree.

Teachers trained to work with three- to six-year-olds are not trained to teach elementary. Elementary teachers are not trained to teach primary. Each level of training has only an overview of the lessons that occur at other levels. For example, as you visit with a primary teacher, he or she will have specific knowledge about primary and only a high level overview and understanding of the elementary curriculum.

To maintain a quality program, schools need to have active recruitment for credentialed teachers. Schools need to budget for training of new credentialed staff. Some Montessori teachers begin as assistants in a class, later obtaining training. Quality programs have ongoing in-service programs offered by experienced Montessori educators. Master teachers mentor new teachers in quality programs, either on- or off-site. Quality schools have periodic external consultation. Each classroom usually has a paraprofessional assistant who commonly is trained in-house for the role of classroom assistant.

Nido: Nido is "nest" in Italian, and the Nido is a Montessori environment designed for the infant between the ages of two months to fourteen months. When the child begins to walk, he or she enters a new environment of the young children's community.

Normalization: The natural or normal state for a human being is characterized by four attributes:

1. A love of work or activity
2. Concentration on an activity
3. Self-discipline
4. Sociability or joyful work

The understanding of normalization doesn't require a leap of faith when you consider those moments when you feel most alive and more "you" than any other time. When we do what we love and love doing it because we have the skill and self-discipline to do the activity well, those are the blissful moments of being human. The activity we love might be anything—chopping wood, singing, dancing, writing, conversing with others, cooking.

In a Montessori school we are trying to help the child attain a natural or normal developmental process, which is referred to as normalization. This process of human development, or normalization, is evident in an observable cycle of activities called normalizing events.

Characteristics of the normalized three- to six-year old:
Love of order
Love of work
Profound spontaneous concentration
Attachment to reality
Love of silence
Love of working alone
Sublimation of possessive instinct
Power to act from real choice
Obedience
Independence and initiative
Spontaneous self-discipline
(*Maria Montessori, Her Life and Work*, E.M. Standing, page 175)

Normalizing Events: In her book *The Secret of Childhood*, Montessori told us of her discovery that, in their natural state, children love to work, which means to be involved in meaningful and purposeful activity.

When we are able to give the child a prepared environment and uninterrupted time to work, the child experiences a "normalizing event."

Children love to be busy, so we prepare their environment with activities that foster a love of work, concentration, self-discipline, and a sense of joyful accomplishment.

There are three steps to a normalizing event:

1. Choose an activity.
2. Complete the activity and return the materials to original order.
3. Have a sense of satisfaction.

In a prepared environment with an uninterrupted, three-hour work cycle, normalizing activities create what Stephen Covey in his book, *The 7 Habits of Highly Effective People*, calls a success cycle. To Montessorians, this process is normalization.

When was your last "normalizing event"? How did it make you feel?

Obstacles: When we come across a barrier to learning, Montessorians refer to that obstruction as an obstacle to development. There are many obstacles in a child's development, and the adult's role is to remove these obstacles whenever possible.

See *Chapter 5, What? No Grades?* for a detailed explanation.

Outdoor Classroom: Most Montessori schools have an outdoor classroom that the children can access as a free choice activity. These outdoor classrooms are usually separate from playground areas for running and other large motor activities. In an ideal situation, the children have direct access to the outdoor classroom from their indoor classroom. In the outdoor classroom, the children can bring selected lessons out and work in the open air. There may be gardening with vegetables and flowers with child-sized tools for digging, raking, shoveling, and hoeing. Children learn to sweep the porches and patios, clean the furniture, and tidy the space as learning activities.

Warmer, more temperate climates are able to use their outdoor classrooms year-round whereas in colder climates use of the outdoor classroom may be limited to favorable weather conditions.

The Montessori outdoor classroom is a vital part of the *prepared environment*. The outdoor classroom becomes the hands-on component of what might be referred to as outdoor education.

Montessorians don't use the term outdoor education as such because it is inherent in the way that we meet the needs of the child through the prepared environment. Whatever words you use, outdoor education is a vital component of Montessori education.

Most schools strive to have a fluid boundary between the outdoors and the indoors whenever possible. Some building designs do not lend themselves to having direct access to the outdoors in every classroom, but those schools usually devise creative solutions for outdoor access.

Learning to take care of the school's outdoor spaces is part of the work of the primary and elementary age child. The elementary child takes this knowledge and goes out into the community to offer community service. The elementary children also begin new outdoor experiences such as camping, hiking, boating, and more.

Parent Education: Parent education in Montessori terms is a series of ongoing lectures, discussions, and demonstrations designed for parents to help bridge the child's world of school and home. Montessorians want to work with the whole child—body, heart, mind, and spirit—and know that what happens at school affects home life and what happens at home affects school life.

Parent education strives to create important home/school and parent/teacher relationships in order to create an optimum environment for the whole child.

Montessori parent education strives to create a strong partnership through mutual understanding and not hearsay.

As a teacher friend of mine tells parents, "If you won't believe everything you hear about school from your child, I promise not to believe everything I hear about home."

Parent education meetings are designed to help you understand your child's development.

Pedagogical Principles: Pedagogy refers to more than just teaching. Montessori pedagogical principles apply to teaching as well as learning. Montessori methods and materials promote learning, fire the child's imagination, and nourish the child's heart and spirit.

Each piece of material and its corresponding lessons have been developed to include the following teaching and learning principles:

- Use of knowledge about human tendencies
- Awareness of psychological characteristics
- Prepared environment
- Limitation of material
- Teacher as link between child and the environment
- Freedom of choice and development of responsibility
- Auto-education or self-construction
- Whole to the parts; concrete to abstract
- The working of the hand and the mind
- Isolation of difficulty
- Observation of the child at work
- Repetition through variety
- Indirect preparation
- Techniques that lead to mental and physical independence

Pedagogical principles are discussed in detail in *Chapter 3, Montessori Principles: More Than Teaching.*

Point of Interest: As the child is learning new skills, the Montessori teacher will repeat a lesson to emphasize a movement or sensorial experience that will help in acquiring that skill.

For example, for the child who forgets to dry his or her hands with a towel, the Montessori teacher may present the hand washing lesson again with a point of interest on the movements and sensation of drying the hands with a towel.

Practical Life: The prepared environment of the primary classroom contains activities that help the child learn dozens of practical self-care skills such as hand washing, dusting, sweeping, clothes washing, and more. The child around the age of three years is extremely interested in these activities. Doing the work with the practical life materials, the child learns to work independently in the classroom and develops concentration. Practical life activities form the foundation for later work with reading and math materials for the four- and five-year-old.

Prepared Environment: We live in a world of prepared environments. Stores, theatres, and restaurants are examples of places that have been prepared to meet specific needs of the user.

A restaurant is prepared to serve our need for food, our need to socialize, and so forth. Wait staff, chefs, and wine stewards are ready to serve us. Tables and chairs are for our comfort and aesthetic appeal. Pictures, flowers, plants, and candles provide decoration.

A good restaurant anticipates our needs. Wait staff offers us drinks and appetizers to make us comfortable. Menu selections are clearly given to us. The restaurant is designed to serve our dining needs, whether it is fast food or a five-star experience.

The prepared environments in a Montessori school are created to meet the developmental needs of children based on observable behaviors; in many ways, it is like a restaurant that is prepared to serve its customers.

There are four basic Montessori environments as follows:
- The infant-toddler environment from birth to age three;
- The primary environment for ages three to six years;
- The elementary environment for ages six to twelve years; and
- The adolescent environments for ages twelve to fifteen and fifteen to eighteen years.

Each Montessori environment is prepared by Montessori-trained people who understand the developmental needs of that age group.

A properly Montessori prepared environment should contain a full complement of *Montessori materials*.

Preschool: Most Montessorians would prefer not to use the word preschool. We prefer to use the term primary to mean the environment and school community for three- to six-year-olds.

In many areas of the United States, primary school means kindergarten through grade six, or for children ages five to twelve years. In order to avoid confusion, many Montessori schools refer to their primary program as preschool when in fact traditional preschools looks nothing like Montessori primary classrooms.

Primary Classroom: Designed for the child between the ages of three to six years, the Montessori primary classroom consists of three components:

1. The physical component of the environment
2. The activities of the children
3. The people involved, or the primary community.

Primary Community: Children age three to six years and adults (including parents) in the primary environment comprise the primary community. If a school has multiple primary classrooms, the term may refer to all the people involved in that age group.

Primary classes in a traditional setting may refer to grades one to six or grades one to three in many parts of the country. Montessorians see the years from three to six being the time of a person's greatest learning and view this period as the *primary* or foundational years of schooling. To Montessorians, there is nothing "pre"-school about this time of children's learning. It is the real deal.

Primary Environment: The primary environment is the prepared environment or classroom for children ages three to six years. The environment usually contains an *outdoor* component as part of the classroom experience.

Psychological Characteristics: For the child from the age of six to twelve years, we refer to the identifying features of that time as psychological characteristics. The child now prefers to do activities with friends instead of working alone. To learn and grow, the elementary age child needs repetition of concepts through a variety of work. For the child in the second plane of development, learning must use the imagination, involve a sense of humor, involve going outside of the familiar school and home, use logic and reason, and exercise the developing sense of right and wrong.

Montessori teachers look for these psychological characteristics in a six-year-old child to see if the child is ready to move into an elementary environment.

Respect for the Child: Montessorians focus on the child's needs and the child's work of creating a unique person. We recognize that the child has a formidable task. We work to be a help to the life of the child, respecting both the person that is not yet there and the one in front of us. This deep respect for the child is considered a major Montessori principle.

Responsibility: The concept of freedom and responsibility is a key idea in the work with children using Montessori philosophy. Freedom follows responsibility. See freedom *and responsibility*.

Self-Construction: The Montessori idea is that the child constructs the adult he or she will become by the self-selected activities the child engages in with concentration, self-discipline, and joyfulness.

This concept of self-construction is perhaps more readily seen with a child's learning to walk and talk. In normal circumstances, we don't have to teach a child how to walk or talk. The child self-constructs as long as the environment is conducive to that building of the person. For example, if a child is confined and not allowed movement, walking will not develop. If a child doesn't hear spoken language, speech will not appear.

In a Montessori classroom, we strive to create a place where children have the freedom to build themselves through self-selected activities in the same way they learned to walk and talk but at a different level involving reading and writing, mathematics, music, science, geography, and practical living activities.

Sensitive Periods: Before the age of six, human beings are in a unique period of learning and development. At this time in our lives, we absorb certain information without conscious effort. Young children learn to walk, talk, and do hundreds of things without formal instruction or being aware of learning. Montessori described these stages as sensitive periods of development, using a term from biologists.

Sensitive periods are characterized by the following five observable behaviors. Children seem to be drawn to certain work, and we see the following:

1. The activity is well-defined with a beginning, middle, and end;
2. The activity is irresistible for the child once he or she starts it;
3. The same activity is returned to again and again;
4. A passionate interest develops; and
5. A restful and tranquil state comes at the finish of the activity.

Once the sensitive period is over, children are not drawn to certain activities as before. Three-year-olds love to wash their hands because they are in a sensitive period for that activity whereas ten-year-olds are not.

There are five basic sensitive periods of development from birth to age six: language, order, refinement of the senses, movement, and social relations.

In the older child, these unique learning periods are called psychological characteristics.

Sensorial Materials: Montessori sensorial materials are self-correcting, hands-on materials to aid your child in developing powers of vision, hearing, touch, taste, and smell.

The sensorial materials engage the hand and the mind to create powerful learning experiences. These experiences become indirect preparation for later academic and artistic skills and create touchstones in the mind for skills such as perfect pitch, color memory, figure memory, and other nonverbal accomplishments.

Visual discernment of length, width, height, and color are addressed through the work with the Pink Tower, Brown Stair, Red Rods, Color Tablets, Cylinder Blocks, and Knobless Cylinders.

The Geometric Cabinet, Geometric Solids, Constructive Triangles, and Binomial and Trinomial Cubes help the child learn different shapes.

Touch is fine-tuned with Rough and Smooth Boards, Fabric Boxes, Mystery Bag, Thermic Bottles, Thermic Tablets, Baric Tablets, and Pressure Cylinders.

Hearing is refined in the work with the Sound Cylinders and the Bell Material along with teacher-initiated sound games.

Tasting activities and the Smelling Bottles help your child distinguish a variety of tastes and aromas.

Each material is designed to help your child's mind focus on a quality, such as color, and distinguish objects by their attributes, which may include color, size, shape, weight, sound, smell, taste, temperature, or other qualities.

Spontaneous Activity: When a child chooses an activity freely in a Montessori classroom and engages with concentration with that chosen activity, this action is referred to as spontaneous activity. This is different from choosing an activity out of curiosity. It connotes the child has passed the curious stage and is using previous knowledge to create new learning.

Structure: Some parents complain that Montessori classrooms are too structured. Others say there is not enough structure.

Traditional preschools are structured around the group changing activities every fifteen or twenty minutes. Snack and recess occur at predictable times each day. For many parents, children being told what to do and being constantly scheduled and entertained by teachers is construed as structure. These parents, therefore, see a Montessori classroom has not having enough structure.

The structure of a Montessori classroom is built on allowing the children free-choice activities in a prepared environment within an uninterrupted three-hour work cycle. Individual work is not interrupted by snack time, song time, or circle time. The child creates an inner structure by having "normalizing events" based on personal interests.

The child entering a Montessori classroom from a traditionally structured preschool may feel anxious by not being told by the teacher what to do every fifteen minutes. It usually takes six to eight weeks for the child to begin to build the inner structure that will give him or her confidence in the Montessori classroom. During this period, a parent may feel that a Montessori classroom is not structured enough.

A parent of a newcomer may think there is too much structure in the classroom when children are asked to use the materials in specific ways. As long as the materials are not being abused or used in a dangerous manner, the children are free to explore the materials *after* they have had an introductory lesson from the teacher.

To the parent of a child in the habit of playing with everything at home without having to consider the effects on other people and surroundings, the Montessori classroom may appear too structured.

An "invisible" structure provided by the process of normalization allows your child to create an internal organization. This self-construction will aid the development of self-discipline that will last a lifetime.

Three-Hour Work Cycle: When given a regular three-hour period, children (and adults) learn to tap into a success cycle. After accomplishing a series of short and familiar tasks in a ninety-minute time frame, a child will choose a task that is challenging and represents challenging and new learning. At this ninety-minute mark, there is a period of restlessness that lasts about ten minutes until the choice for the challenging activity is made. The new activity may last for sixty to ninety minutes.

At the end of a work cycle, it is not unusual to see a child in quiet satisfaction smiling both outwardly and inwardly.

Toddler: Toddler refers to the children who have begun to walk and are in the young children's communities for children ages fourteen to thirty-six months.

Upper Elementary: The upper elementary is for children about ages nine to twelve years of age. See *elementary environment.*

Whole Child: In the process of aiding development, Montessorians focus on the growth of the whole child, not just academics. The paradox of focusing on the development of the whole child, through the process of normalization, is that academic interest and skills bloom as the child develops a habit of learn-commit-do, or a success cycle.

Montessorians are concerned with overall development of the whole person—body, mind, heart, and spirit. Our challenge is that we must model the self-discipline, the vision, the passion, and the conscience that is at the heart of true learning and self-discovery for our children. The child is more than a being learning how to read, write, and do arithmetic.

As Montessorians and adults, we walk with our children a path of trust, helping them to understand how to live their lives, how to develop their talents, how to share their love, and how to do what's right. Corrections on our path should strive to be of loving intention to serve the needs of the whole child, not just the academic aspects of the child's work.

Work: Purposeful activity is called work. Montessori observed that children learn by engaging in purposeful activity of their own choosing. When children can choose what they do, they do not differentiate between work and play.

Work Cycle: A basic work cycle begins with choosing an activity, doing that activity, returning the activity to order, and then experiencing a sense of satisfaction. That defines one unit or cycle of work.

This sense of satisfaction, which may last a few seconds to a few minutes, helps motivate the child (and adult) to choose the next activity, thus creating another cycle of work.

As the child matures, his or her work cycle will grow until the child is able to maintain a three-hour level of activity. True learning occurs during the last ninety minutes of the three-hour work cycle when a child, after experiencing satisfaction with previous work, will choose a new and challenging activity to master.

This all begins with the child choosing, doing, returning to order, feeling satisfaction, then choosing again. Each activity contributes to an upward spiral of successful learning within the child.

Five-year-olds in a Montessori classroom usually begin to establish a second three-hour work cycle in the afternoon.

The development of a work cycle is an important component in the idea of normalization for the child. In our Montessori schools, every day we should try to protect a three-hour work period from interruption in order for the child to develop a three-hour work cycle.

An interesting piece of work, freely chosen, which has the virtue of inducing concentration rather than fatigue, adds to the child's energies and mental capacities, and leads him to self-mastery.

Maria Montessori

The Absorbent Mind, page 188

Work Journal: In the elementary classroom, the children keep a work journal or work diary of their daily activities. This journal helps the child become more aware of how he or she spends his or her time as well as serves as a record of lessons given and work done. The journal is often written in a spiral-bound steno pad. This journal becomes more sophisticated and detailed as the child matures. A page from a six-year-old's journal follows:

Sample of elementary students work journal

Tuesday, January 15, 2008

8:00	am	Arrive/Outside
8:30	am	Class meeting
8:45	am	Lesson with squares of numbers 1 to 10
9:15	am	snack
9:45	am	draw squares
11:00	am	make poster of squares
11:30	am	clean up/outside/lunch
12:30	pm	listen to "Secret Garden"
1:00	pm	grammar box II
1:30	pm	work on time line of life
2:30	pm	draw picture/story
3:00	pm	go home

Work is love made visible.
Kahlil Gibran
The Prophet, page 33

Dr. Maria Montessori, 1933

Resources

Child-sized Materials

When my daughters were little, everything child-sized had to be special ordered or custom built. Finding affordable, quality, child-sized tables and chairs was not possible for us, and my husband built our daughters' table and easel. Fortunately, today's discount stores, such as Wal-Mart, Target, and many others, offer affordable and attractive child-sized tables and chairs along with child-sized gardening tools, brooms, and other practical items for children's activities.

Here are my three favorite catalog stores where I have ordered real tools for young children for many years.

Montessori Services/ For Small Hands

MontessoriServices.com
Montessori Services
1 West Barham Avenue
Santa Rosa, CA 95407

Montessori Services offers small pitchers, trays, baskets, brooms, gardening tools, and other materials to help children work and play at home. To order a catalog, call Montessori Services Customer Service: 877-975-3003 or 707-579-3003 Monday through Friday, 8:00 a.m. to 4:30 p.m. (PST).

Michael Olaf Montessori Company

MichaelOlaf.com

Michael Olaf Montessori Company

65 Ericson Court, #1

Arcata, California 95521

The Michael Olaf Company has materials to use with children from birth through age twelve, offered in two catalogs, *The Joyful Child* for children from birth to age three, and *Child of the World* for children from the ages of three to twelve years.

In addition, the Michael Olaf Company catalog offers a variety of beautiful learning materials for science, math, biology, art, language, music, and more. There is a downloadable catalog on their Web site, but they do not offer online ordering.

To order a catalog, call their free number 888-880-9235.

Lakeshore Learning

LakeshoreLearning.com

Lakeshore Learning Materials

2695 E. Dominguez St.

Carson, CA 90895

Lakeshore Learning offers educational materials for early childhood and elementary-aged children. They offer classroom-sized quantities, but they also offer items individually. At Lakeshore it may not be possible to order a single broom, though you can order a Super Cleaning Set that has a kitchen broom, a porch broom, a dust mop, a wet mop, a whisk brush, and a dustpan, all on a wooden holder.

If you are into arts and crafts, Lakeshore has fun items as well as practical ones. The washable tempera is one of my favorite practical items.

To order a free catalog, call 1-800-778-4456 Monday through Friday 6:00, a.m. to 6:00 p.m. and Saturday, 8:30 a.m. to 5:00 p.m. (PST) or order online.

Montessori-Based Books for Parents

Britton, Lesley. *Montessori Play and Learn* (Three Rivers Press) 1992.

ISBN 0-517-59182-0

Practical advice to make your home a wonderful place of learning and activity for your children.

Gettman, David. *Basic Montessori: Learning Activities for Under-Fives* (St. Martin's Griffin) 1987.

ISBN 0-312-01864-9

An overview with instructions of learning activities for young children that includes practical life skills, language, cultural, and mathematics presentations

Hainstock, Elizabeth. Teaching Montessori in the Home: The Pre-School Years (A Plume Book) 1968, 1997.

ISBN 0-452-27909-7

A presentation guide for giving Montessori-style lessons in the home.

Lawrence, Lynne. *Montessori Read and Write* (Three Rivers Press) 1998.

ISBN 0-609-80335-2

A comprehensive explanation and how-to book to help your child learn to read and write using Montessori philosophy and learning techniques.

Seldin, Tim. *How to Raise an Amazing Child the Montessori Way* (DK Publishing) 2006.

ISBN 978-0-7566-2505-4

A beautifully illustrated and very approachable guide for systematic and comprehensive parenting using Montessori philosophy.

Seldin, Tim and Epstein, Paul. *The Montessori Way.* (The

Montessori Foundation Press) 2003.

ISBN 0-9746387-0-6

A comprehensive handbook for the Montessori parent. Montessori materials are explained and Montessori principles are covered. With wonderful photographs, it's a book you'll enjoy having on your coffee table.

Wolf, Aline. *A Parent's Guide to the Montessori Classroom* (Parent-Child Press) 1980.

No ISBN

This sixty-two-page book describes the Montessori materials for the three- to six-year-old. The materials and lessons are well described and illustrated with black-and-white photos. This is a book that each of our new families received at my school.

Other Recommended Books

Included here are books, in alphabetical order by author, that I have found useful in my understanding of the young child and human development.

Covey, Stephen R. *The Seven Habits of Highly Effective Families* (St. Martin's Griffin) 1998.

ISBN 0-307440850

Covey takes his *Seven Habits* and puts it in a form for us to use in our families.

Dyer, Wayne W. *What Do You Really Want for Your Children?* (Quill) 1985.

ISBN 0-380-73047-2

"Straightforward, commonsense advice that no parent can afford to do without," is on the cover, and I couldn't agree more.

Faber, Adele and Elaine Mazlish. *How to Talk So Kids Will Listen and Listen So Kids Will Talk* (Avon Books) 1980.

ISBN 0-380-57000-9

Practical how-to advice for understanding your children.

Glennon, Will. *200 Ways to Raise a Boy's Emotional Intelligence* (Conari Press) 2000.

ISBN 1-57324-020-6

A small book full of big ideas of how to strengthen emotional skills and express emotions.

Goleman, Daniel. *Emotional Intelligence* (Bantam Books) 1995.

ISBN 0-553-09503-X

This groundbreaking book shows why a high emotional intelligence quotient, EQ, may be more important than a high intelligence quotient, IQ.

Gottman, John. *Raising an Emotionally Intelligent Child* (A Fireside Book) 1998.

ISBN 0-684-83865-6

A guide to teaching children about their emotions and connecting heart, hand, and mind.

Hannaford, Carla. *Smart Moves: Why Learning Is Not All in Your Head* (Great Ocean Publishers) 1995.

ISBN 0-915556-27-8

Hannaford explains how the brain and body work together and gives information on Brain Gym.

Healy, Jane M. *Your Child's Growing Mind* (Broadway) 1987, 1994.

ISBN 0-385-46930-6

A look at brain development from birth through adolescence.

Jensen, Eric. *Enriching the Brain: How To Maximize Every Learner's Potential.* (Jossey-Bass) 2006.

ISBN 978-0-470-22389-5

Jensen gives practical ways to use the latest brain research.

Levine, Mel. *A Mind at a Time* (Simon and Schuster) 2002.

ISBN 0-7432-0223-6

An overview of how humans learn and the importance of becoming your child's "mind-watcher."

Medina, John. *Brain Rules* (Pear Press) 2008.

ISBN 0979777704

Medina gives us twelve brain principles to help us thrive and survive school, work, home and play.

Seligman, Martin E. P. *The Optimistic Child* (Houghton Mifflin) 1995.

ISBN 0-06-097709-4

Foster true self-esteem by teaching your children how to play, think, argue, and express their feelings effectively.

Montessori Professional Organizations

This list of Montessori organizations presents what I consider to be the most influential and important Montessori organizations active in the United States.

Association Montessori International (AMI and AMI/USA)

The Association Montessori International is the oldest Montessori organization, established in 1929 by Dr. Montessori to maintain the integrity of her work. AMI provides teacher training and school accreditation. Visit their web site at: *Amiusa.org*

American Montessori Society (AMS)

American Montessori Society was founded in 1960 to promote Montessori education "within the context of the American culture." Today, the AMS is the largest Montessori organization in the world, with more than 10,000 members, including some outside the America. Like the AMI, the AMS also provides teacher training and school accreditation, though the two organizations' training and accreditation requirements differ. Visit the AMS web site at: *Amshq.org*

I belong to both these organizations and know them to work diligently to bring Montessori philosophy, methods and materials to children.

The Montessori Foundation and *the International Montessori Council (IMC)*

The Montessori Foundation was established in 1992 to create an independent, unaffiliated source of assistance for the international Montessori community. The Montessori Foundation works with the entire Montessori professional community, as well as with parents, to facilitate understanding of the work of Dr. Montessori.

In 1998, The Montessori Foundation organized an independent membership organization, The International Montessori Council, which offers school accreditation, professional development for teachers and school administrators. At the time of this book's publication, the Montessori Foundation and the IMC share their website; visit it at: *Montessori.org*

I also belong to The Montessori Foundation and the IMC. They are outstanding organizations, committed to promoting Montessori philosophy and practices.

AMI, AMS and IMC each sponsor multiple professional conferences each year, however AMI conferences are usually open to only those who hold AMI certification.

North America Montessori Teachers Association (NAMTA)

The North America Montessori Teachers Association focuses on teacher development. It is an affiliate organization of AMI. NAMTA-sponsored conferences are open to parents. Visit their web site at: *Montessori-namta.org*

Montessori Accreditation Council for Teacher Education (MACTE)

The Montessori Accreditation Council for Teacher Education is an autonomous accrediting agency for Montessori teacher training programs. As noted, MACTE is autonomous and not affiliated with any Montessori professional organizations. MACTE strives to create standards to assure high-quality training for teachers. Montessori teachers trained in a MACTE accredited program can be expected to have a comprehensive understanding of Montessori principles, methods and materials. Visit their web site at: *Macte.org*

Montessori Bibliography

First Things First

A young lady in her mid-twenties, herself a product of a Montessori education and now a business manager, told me that the beauty of Montessori schools is that parents don't have to read anything written by Dr. Montessori for their children to do fabulously in a Montessori school. She said, "All they have to do is look at their children and see how happy they are."

For those who would like to read some of Dr. Montessori's writings, I've listed her books with a short summary. Dr. Montessori's books developed from speeches and essays, and for the most part each chapter is a stand-alone unit, building on each other.

My first Montessori read was *The Absorbent Mind*, and it tends to be the book I recommend as a beginning. *The Absorbent Mind*, *The Secret of Childhood*, and *The Discovery of the Child* make most people's top three list for first-time readings.

I find reading Dr. Montessori's work a little like reading other writing from the turn of the 1900s. Mix H. G. Wells with a passionate, Catholic Italian scientist and you have what today might be considered ornate oratory, but the story is marvelous.

Over the years, I've found Dr. Montessori's words insightful, inspirational, and worth the effort. I would wish the same for you.

The quotes from Dr. Montessori used in this book come from the editions listed in this bibliography.

Books by Dr. Maria Montessori

The Absorbent Mind (ABC-Clio Ltd.) Oxford, England: 1949, 1988.
ISBN 1-85109-087-8

This volume of Dr. Montessori's work is based on lectures given in her first training course after World War II and after her internment in India. (A historical note: Being Italian, Dr. Montessori was interned in India during World War II, but was allowed to continue to train teachers during those years.)

Dr. Montessori discusses the development of infants and young children from birth to three years and includes information about the process of normalization and the three levels of obedience. This was my first of Dr. Montessori's books to read. 270 pages.

The Advanced Montessori Method, Volumes 1 and 2 (ABC-Clio Ltd.) Oxford, England: 1918, 1991.

Volume 1: ISBN 1-85109-114-9

Volume 2: ISBN 1-85109-233-1

Volume 1 is a collection of nine essays including both theory and practice at the primary elementary levels. These include the following: "A Survey of the Child's Life," "A Survey of Modern Education," "My Contribution to Experimental Science," "The Preparation of the Teacher," "Environment," "Attention," "Will," "Intelligence," and "Imagination."

Volume 2 is an overview of the lessons Dr. Montessori developed. This volume was published first in 1916 and is probably of more historical interest to Montessori enthusiasts. The information in this volume shows the foundations of all the later lessons developed. It still contains valuable insights. Lessons in grammar, reading, arithmetic, geometry, drawing, music, and poetry metrics are explained.

The Child in the Family (ABC-Clio Ltd.) Oxford, England: 1975, 1989.

ISBN 1-85109-113-0

This is a short book of eleven essays on human development, beginning with newborn child and including the adult. It's the type of book, as are many of Dr. Montessori's books, where reading a short essay a day provides a nice balance of inspiration and contemplation. 75 pages.

The Discovery of the Child (Ballantine Books) New York: 1967.

ISBN 0-345-33656-9

This book contains early writings of Dr. Montessori (updated in 1948) highlighting the materials and the works of the child in primary class, ages three to six. 339 pages.

Education and Peace (ABC-Clio Ltd.) Oxford, England: 1949, 1972, 1992.

ISBN 1-85109-168-8 S

This book is a collection of speeches Montessori gave in the 1930s. The foundations for peace, how to educate for peace, and the importance of education for peace are discussed in fifteen essays. 119 pages.

Education for a New World (ABC-Clio Ltd.) Oxford, England: 1989.

ISBN 1-85109-095-9

This book deals with the role of education in a changing world. Some see this book as a shorter presentation of *The Absorbent Mind*, and many of the same issues are discussed. 77 pages.

The Formation of Man (ABC-Clio Ltd.) Oxford, England: 1989.

ISBN 1-85109-097-5

These five essays were originally published in India in 1955. This book includes material concerning Dr. Montessori's approach to world literacy and world peace. 116 pages.

From Childhood to Adolescence (ABC-Clio Ltd.) Oxford, England: 1948, 1994.

This book addresses the development and education of the child from age seven through adolescence. Includes *Erdkinder* and "The Function of the University." 93 pages.

The Secret of Childhood (Ballantine Books) New York: 1966.

Dr. Montessori's book told the world of the child's natural, spontaneous urge to learn. This secret of childhood became the foundation of Dr. Montessori's lifetime of work with children. This book provides an introduction, both practical and theoretical, including observations and insights into the nature of young children. 216 pages.

To Educate the Human Potential (ABC-Clio Ltd.) Oxford, England: 1948, 1989.

ISBN 1-85109-094-0

This book outlines the needs of the elementary age child regarding the acquisition of culture and the understanding of history as the story of mankind, all in the context of showing the child the universe. Cosmic Education is introduced in this volume. 85 pages.

What You Should Know about Your Child (ABC-Clio Ltd.) Oxford, England: 1961, 1989.

The book is a collection of lectures that focus on the development of the child. The series of twenty-one essays are short and are perfect for a daily dose of information and inspiration. 99 pages.

By Mario Montessori

The Human Tendencies and Montessori Education (AMI, Second Edition).

A classical essay on the imagination, the natural characteristics of the child, and the integration of human development and history. 12 pages.

By Mario M. Montessori, Jr.

Education for Human Development (ABC-Clio Ltd.) Oxford, England: 1976, 1992.

This is a series of eight lectures given by Dr. Montessori's grandson, Mario. They deal with the ideas of Montessori from a philosophical, psychological, and educational point of view. Foreword by Buckminster Fuller. 114 pages.

By E.M. Standing

Maria Montessori: Her Life and Work (Penguin Books) New York: 1957, 1984.

This book is a biography, including Dr. Montessori's life, her development of material, the child's work in the class, and the growth of the Montessori movement.

By Paula Polk Lillard

Montessori—A Modern Approach (Schocken) New York: 1972, 1988.

ISBN 0805209204

Paula Polk Lillard has written four books about Montessori philosophy and education. *Montessori—A Modern Approach* introduces a history of Dr. Montessori and the origins of her educational method. Montessori philosophy is explained using many quotes from Montessori's books. One section deals with the role of parents in a child's development. The Montessori approach to writing and reading is explained as well as why Montessori is pertinent today more than ever. 192 pages.

Lillard's other books (see below) are probably best after reading this first volume.

Montessori Today: A Comprehensive Approach to Education from Birth to Adulthood (Schocken) New York: 1996.
ISBN 080521061X

Montessori from the Start: The Child at Home, from Birth to Age Three (Schocken) New York: 2003. Note: This was written with Lynn Lillard Jessen.
ISBN 0805211128

Montessori in the Classroom: A Teacher's Account of How Children Really Learn (Schocken) New York: 1997.
ISBN 0805210873

By Angeline Stoll Lillard, Ph.D.

Montessori: The Science Behind the Genius (Oxford University Press) New York: 2005.

ISBN 0-19-51868-6

Lillard, in the preface, writes that twenty years ago she was a Montessori skeptic. But her work in developmental psychology showed that the central tenets of Montessori are supported by a strong body of evidence, for example, sensitive periods of development.

Lillard, Montessori trained and the daughter of Paula Polk Lillard, brings together the theory and the practice to make Montessori educational thinking and evidence accessible to researchers. For those who prefer verifiable research in their decision making, Lillard's book will help establish the scientific basis in modern terms.

This is not the first book I'd suggest to someone new to Montessori education, but if you are a skeptic with a desire to understand the scientific basis of the Montessori method and find the most effective educational method, read this book.

For others less research inclined, you might enjoy watching the video of the same name, which is a lecture given to a parent group by Lillard.

Visit Dr. Lillard's website at: *Montessori-science.org*

By Kathleen H. Futtrell

The Normalized Child (North American Montessori Teacher's Association) Burton, Ohio: 1998.

No ISBN. Available at Montessori-namta.org.

This twenty-eight page booklet is filled with beautiful pictures and inspiration about the normal development of the child. The booklet originated as a parent talk. Each entering family into my school received a copy of this booklet. It is magazine-sized and is perfect for keeping on your reading table at home for inspiration.

Dr. Montessori's Book Chapters by Subject

This is a compilation of Dr. Montessori's book chapters by subject. I've found this list useful and thought readers of this book might too.

Arithmetic
The Discovery of the Child
Chapter 18: Arithmetic
Chapter 19: More Arithmetic

Care of the Newborn
The Absorbent Mind
Chapter 4: The New Path
Chapter 5: The Miracle of Creation
Chapter 9: The First Day of Life
The Child in the Family
Chapter 1: The Blank Page
Chapter 2: The Newborn Child
Chapter 3: The Spiritual Embryo

Discipline
The Absorbent Mind
Chapter 24: Mistakes and Their Correction
Chapter 25: The Three Levels of Obedience
Chapter 26: Discipline and the Teacher
The Advanced Montessori Method, Volume I
Chapter 6: Attention
Chapter 7: Will
The Discovery of the Child
Chapter 23: Discipline in a Children's House
The Secret of Childhood
Chapter 30: The Rights of the Child, The Mission of Parents
What You Should Know about Your Child
Chapter 20: Work and Discipline

Education
The Advanced Montessori Method, Volume I
Chapter 1: A Survey of the Child's Life
Chapter 2: A Survey of Modern Education
Chapter 8: Intelligence

Geography
To Educate the Human Potential
The entire book

Imagination
The Absorbent Mind
Chapter 17: Through Culture and Imagination
The Advanced Montessori Method, Volume I
Chapter 9: Imagination
To Educate the Human Potential
Chapter 2: The Right Use of Imagination

Importance of the First Three Years
The Absorbent Mind
Chapter 6: Embryology and Behavior
Chapter 7: The Spiritual Embryo
The Secret of Childhood
Chapter 6: The Spiritual Embryo
What You Should Know about Your Child
Chapter 6: The First Three Years

Language, Spoken
The Absorbent Mind
Chapter 10: Some Thoughts on Language
Chapter 11: How Language Calls to the Child
The Discovery of the Child
Chapter 17: Speech
What You Should Know about Your Child
Chapter 8: Language

Language, Written
The Discovery of the Child
Chapter 14: Written Language
Chapter 15: The Mechanisms of Writing
Chapter 16: Reading
What You Should Know about Your Child
Chapter 17: Written Language and Human Progress

Observation
The Advanced Montessori Method, Volume I
Chapter 3: My Contribution to Experimental Science

Obstacles to Development
The Absorbent Mind
Chapter 12: The Effect of Obstacles on Development
Chapter 18: Character and Its Defects in Childhood
Chapter 20: Character Building is the Child's Own Achievement
The Secret of Childhood
Chapter 10: Obstacles to Growth
Chapter 23: Deviations
Chapter 24: Repercussions on Physical Health

Peace
Education and Peace
The entire book

Periods of Development
The Absorbent Mind
Chapter 3: The Periods of Growth
What You Should Know about Your Child
Chapter 4: Natural Laws of Development
Chapter 5: Periods of Development

Also see "Importance of the First Three Years."

Personality and Character Development
The Absorbent Mind
Chapter 12: The Effect of Obstacles on Development
Chapter 18: Character and Its Defects in Childhood
Chapter 20: Character Building is the Child's Own Achievement
The Child in the Family
Chapter 7: The Character of the Child
The Secret of Childhood
Chapter 14: The Substitution of the Personality
Chapter 25: The Conflict Between Adult and Child
Chapter 28: The Guiding Instincts
What You Should Know about Your Child
Chapter 12: The Happiness of Achievement
Chapter 13: The Key to Mental Health and Growth

Preparation of the Environment
The Advanced Montessori Method, Volume I
Chapter 5: Environment
The Child in the Family
Chapter 8: The Child's Environment
What You Should Know about Your Child
Chapter 14: The Camera and the Crystal

Also see "The Task of the Teacher."

Primary School (for three- to six-year-olds)
The Discovery of the Child
Appendix: Inaugural Address, page 330

Religious Education
The Discovery of the Child
Chapter 22: Religious Education

Sensitive Periods
The Secret of Childhood
Chapter 7: Psychic Development

Sensorial Education
The Discovery of the Child
Chapter 6: The Material for Development
Chapter 8: Visual and Auditory Distinctions
Chapter 9: On the Training of the Senses

Social Development
The Absorbent Mind
Chapter 21: Children's Possessiveness and its
Transformations
Chapter 22: Social Development
Chapter 23: Cohesion in the Social Unit

Task of the Teacher
The Absorbent Mind
Chapter 27: The Teacher's Preparation
The Advanced Montessori Method, Volume I
Chapter 4: The Preparation of the Teacher
The Child in the Family
Chapter 10: The New Teacher
Chapter 11: The Adult and the Child
The Discovery of the Child
Chapter 3: Teaching Methods Employed in Children's
Houses

Acknowledgements

I wish to thank my husband, Mark, for encouraging me to expand a magazine article into a book. His technical guidance helped me complete something this century.

My daughters, Dana and Hannah, have been my cheerleaders in this project, as they understand the benefits of a Montessori education.

A big thank you to my parents, Don and Sharon Stark, and to the rest of my family, who always believed I could do anything.

Thank you to Tim Seldin, president of the Montessori Foundation, and to the staff of *Tomorrow's Child* magazine for printing book excerpts, showing me that this book was possible.

Thanks to Sharon Caldwell and Sharon Padgett for reading the first proof and offering their insights.

I value Anita August, Sharon Schmidt and Hannah Schmidt reading through the second proof and offering their comments.

I appreciate my dear friend, Debbie Potochnik, for final editing assistance.

And a final thanks to you, the reader.

About the Authors

Maren Stark Schmidt

Maren Schmidt currently writes an award-winning newspaper column on child development issues, Kids Talk. She is a certified Association Montessori Internationale (AMI) elementary practitioner. Ms. Schmidt founded a Montessori school in 1991 and has over twenty-five years experience working with children.

During those years Schmidt taught children, from ages two to fifteen years, acting as school administrator, curriculum coordinator, and parent education coordinator, as well as being a classroom teacher. She has also worked for several years as a parenting instructor using the *Active Parenting* curriculum.

Schmidt holds a M.Ed. in Curriculum and Instruction from Loyola College in Baltimore, Maryland. She attended the University of Arkansas at Little Rock, earning a degree in Interpersonal and Organizational Communications.

Schmidt resides in Welches, Oregon with her husband, Mark. She is the mother of two daughters, Dana and Hannah.

At present, Schmidt divides her professional time between writing, speaking and consulting on Montessori and child development topics. Visit MarenSchmidt.com for more information.

Dana Cone Schmidt

Dana Schmidt was a Montessori student from age one to fourteen years. A graduate of Dartmouth College, Dana currently works as an international account manager for a biomedical firm in San Francisco.

About the Illustrator

Syd Kruse

Syd Kruse is a watercolorist living in Zigzag, Oregon with her husband Steve, daughter, Kiki, and son, Dan.

CPSIA information can be obtained at www.ICGtesting.com
Printed in the USA
242030LV00003B/3/P